Form Si

A Guide To
Pedigree Handicapping
by Lawrence Taylor

To Deb
Whose belief and support have helped me
to realise one of my life goals.

With many thanks to Raceform, Kathleen Jones,
Tim Drakeford, and everyone else who gave their
assistance.

Published by Raceform Limited, Compton,
Newbury, Berkshire RG20 6NL
Tel: 01635 578080 Fax: 01635 578101
Web: www.raceform.co.uk
Email: raceform@raceform.co.uk

CONTENTS

Form Sires

Introduction

It was on a rainy night at Monmore Green back in the late seventies that I first became aware of a link between breeding and performance. In those days I followed greyhound racing almost religiously and attended Monmore Green, Perry Barr and Willenhall whenever I could. This was a particularly miserable night, with the track only surfacing occasionally from under giant pools of water. Racing really should have been abandoned, but they kept the show on the road if only to satisfy the small crowd of wet, cold, but extremely dedicated racegoers.

The memory of that night has stayed with me for one reason. Three of the winners on the card were litter brothers. And I remember wondering if their father or mother had also been gifted with the ability to walk on water. It was obvious that most of the competing animals that night just couldn't handle the conditions, yet the litter brothers raced and won with little apparent effort.

A few years later, as my attentions turned to matters equine, I began to note the pedigrees of horses who had won first time out. I found that some sires of first-time winners on the Flat were also able to produce first time out novice hurdle winners. This led to many a 'coup' being landed during the early months of each jump season, especially if the animals under investigation had previously shown some ability on the Flat.

Today, with the arrival of faster computers and complementary racing software, I'm able to study the relationship between breeding and performance in much more detail. Sire research that used to take hours, days, or weeks, can now be accomplished in a matter of minutes, which encourages me to ask more and more questions - and so back I go to the computer. It's a deliciously vicious circle.

If you want to take your racing seriously, and improve your chances of betting success, then the study of pedigree handicapping will enable you to stay ahead of the crowd. It's a brand new approach to the game that will come to feature prominently in the minds of horseplayers in years to come, and its growing popularity will mean greater exposure in the racing press.

I am grateful to *Raceform* for allowing me to produce this book under their banner. Their good name will help bring some credibility to a subject matter which is all too readily ignored by horseplayers, and often scoffed at by high-minded breeding experts. Pedigree handicapping should be of importance to both horseplayers and breeding experts alike, for both are in search of the same thing - WINNERS.

Form Sires

Form Sires

Chapter 1

Pedigree Handicapping

What is Pedigree Handicapping?

Pedigree Handicapping (PH) is the use of breeding as a winner-finding tool. You may have used it yourself without even realising it. For example, how many of us have looked more favourably on the chances of a horse by Risk Me when there is give in the ground? Or nodded sagely to ourselves when we discover that our selection, a two-year-old running over ten furlongs, is by the stamina-giving sire Ela-Mana-Mou? On each occasion we are making a positive mental note and bringing into play pedigree handicapping at its simplest level.

We can make the above assumptions about the progeny of Risk Me and Ela-Mana-Mou because we have studied the racecourse performances of their previous offspring. From this body of evidence we are able to identify traits which are being handed down from one generation to the other. These traits can either be positive (such as an ability to carry weight), or negative (such as an inability to handle soft ground), but either way, these traits can be harnessed for profit.

The saying 'horses for courses' contains more than a small measure of truth. It underlines the fact that horses are to be relied upon if given conditions which favour their physical and mental attributes. Identifying these attributes, or traits, and attaching meaningful numbers to them, is what pedigree handicapping is all about.

Traits are easy to identify using simple mathematics. For example, if I were to enter the sire Last Tycoon into my *Computer Raceform* database and run it, we'd find that his progeny won 119 of their 1,061 races over a four-year period on the Flat. This equates to an overall strike rate (OSR) of 11.22%. Now, if we run the program again, only this time stipulate that it only considers runners carrying 9 stone 7 pounds or over in their races, we'd find that 19 of the 117 qualifiers had won, which would equate to a strike rate of 16.24%. This would show that the progeny of Last Tycoon make excellent weight carriers as they win 1.45 times more often when carrying the extra burden (16.24 divided by 11.22 = 1.45 (rounded)). Any number above 1 would be regarded as a positive result, while numbers less than 1 (such as 0.32) indicate a negative result under rule (the 'rule' in this case being that progeny must carry 9-7 or more in their races).

Some sceptics may think that pedigree handicapping is a bit like shooting in the dark, in that any 'hits' are likely to be the result of pure chance more than anything else. But while agreeing that nothing is certain when analysing the pedigrees of racehorses (let alone attaching meaningful numbers to them) I think it is safe to say that there is enough consistency within the breed for pedigree handicapping to have a significant role to play.

Waiting for breeding information to drip from the pen of some race-weary hack is all very well, but most serious horseplayers need more than a trickle of facts if their curiosity is to be satisfied. Some players are canny enough to take on board what has been let slip so far, and project forward to a time when many of the great handicapping mysteries will be solved using this method. Now, with the arrival of the information age, they have the opportunity to explore the relationship between breeding and form for themselves.

Most interestingly, there are no set rules as to how to apply pedigree handicapping to the task of picking winners. Speed figure analysis, for example, can and does follow a fairly structured path (racetimes/standard times/going allowance/speed figs), but not so PH. With this unique tool we can be as simplistic or as complex as we like, and the resulting data will, more likely than not, differ from that proffered by other PHDs (Pedigree Handicapping Disciples).

You may be asking why PH is not already widely used by today's horseplayers. After all, if it is such a potent weapon to use against the bookmakers then why isn't it already receiving maximum exposure via the racing media?

Well, here are some reasons why pedigree handicapping continues to be racing's greatest secret.

The Competition:

Other forms of winner-finding, such as form and speed, have come to dominate the pages of the racing press and, therefore, the thinking of most horseplayers. A good many racing editors would probably love to include all manner of breeding information on their pages, but their hands are tied because of lack of space. How many editors would kick out a £500 advertisement so that some kooky PHD could have his say on the merits of Beveled's progeny over the minimum trip at Yarmouth.

The truth? Err.. Not many.

Form:

The Form Book has been our Bible for so long that many would think it sacrilege if asked to evaluate racehorse performance in any other way. It is something we are used to and something we care about (even if, on the odd occasion, we feel the need to throw it out of the window). We don't like change, so we stick

Form Sires

with what we know, and, on balance, it does a good enough job to persuade most people that it is the number one truth-giver.

Speed:

Americans do not believe in form, but they will readily fall to their knees in the praise of SPEED. Because of the nature of their racing (fast from the gate to get a good position on their tight tracks), and because they use something that UK racing is only just adopting (sectional timing), speed means everything. And, like most things from the other side of the pond, speed has arrived in the UK with a vengeance. Not yet ready to topple form from its lofty perch, speed is gaining acceptability here, and even I must confess to being one of its followers.

Trainer Methods:

What I know about trainer methods you could write on the back of a stamp, but that does not mean I don't respect those who pay very particular attention to this aspect of the game. I realise that it must provide a valuable edge to many horseplayers, but it is just something I have not had the time to investigate fully, though it rightly gets plenty of space in the racing press.

Systems:

Some systemites gain a great deal from the study of systems. At its best system-building helps the horseplayer investigate many facets of the sport, with knowledge creeping in at every turn. But at its worst it can be THE number one reason why they don't bother to learn about the true dynamics of the game.

O.K. I have explained why pedigree handicapping is not on the agenda of most horseplayers (or editors) so maybe it's time I gave some reasons why it should be.

The Value Of Pedigree Handicapping:

In theory it should be possible to select a 'dead cert' for the Brocklesby Stakes using PH. Which is pretty damn good considering the race takes place on the first day of the Flat racing season, and is contested by unraced two-year-olds! In other words, a horse selected by PH does not have to have previously encountered its racing environment. It just has to have good supporting evidence from the previous racing exploits of its sires progeny.

Sudden changes in the going, or horses stepping up in distance, can often leave bettors scratching their heads. They will anticipate the probability of a big turnaround in form, yet few will bother to look to breeding for the answers. Those

7

who do will find a resource that is almost as profitable as having (genuine) inside information.

Because so few horseplayers pay attention to breeding as a winner-finding tool, it follows that horses who are selected using this method are likely to start at odds greater than they should be. Most players will concentrate on horses with superior form and/or speed figures, shortening up the odds on such animals and extending them on those horses who head the breeding stats. PH is one area of the game where giant overlays can often be found.

Money matters aside, PH is a great subject to study in its own right. It can take you to the very roots of the game and help you to respect racehorses as unique individuals, rather than expecting them to perform like machines just because the money is down. Don't be afraid that the study of PH will be too difficult, or that it is so dry that only a librarian (archive section) would find it of interest. If you are a creative thinker (and half decent at maths) then the rest is down to your own commitment and enthusiasm.

Tools Of The Trade:

For those of you who want to take the study of pedigree handicapping seriously, I would suggest that you invest in a computer and the relevant racing software. You can approach this task without the aid of both, but you will be taking a much slower route, and keeping track of all the information will be that much more difficult.

A decent computer will set you back around £1,000, and for this you will get all the speed and capacity you need. That is, the machine will be fast enough to churn through the racing data at an acceptable rate, and the hard disk will be big enough for you to store as many racing software packages as you require.

The two racing software packages I have used for this book are: *Computer Raceform* (for the bulk of the work), and Racing System Builder (for the analysis of damsires). These packages are not cheap, but they are a great investment. Not only will they enable you to increase your learning curve sharply, they will also save you a great deal of time. Manually thumbing through form/breeding books is now almost as unacceptable as smoking in a public place. So, if at all possible, beg, steal or borrow a computer.

The next step (after not owning, and then owning a computer) is to get the thing hooked up to the Internet. For around £10 a month, plus call charges, you can access a hell of a lot of racing and breeding information. You will also be able to contact other racing enthusiasts via e-mail, and even put up your own Web pages for the world to see. Most of the large racing organisations are on the Internet -

Form Sires

including *Raceform* and Weatherbys. The latter offering subscribers (at £18 per month) all manner of breeding information, such as a three-generation pedigree of all horses in training, which, for the breeding enthusiast, is a bit like having a birthday every day.

I must admit that all of this can add up to a fair bit of money, so, if you are on a tight budget, why not compile your own breeding database? This way you can forget about racing software and linking up to the Internet, and just go out and buy a reasonably priced computer - say £500 worth, enter the details of winners onto a database (including names of sires and damsires etc.) and then, when enough information has accumulated, conduct your own research and analysis. I do this myself (even though I own some nifty racing software) and find the exercise very rewarding. One thing's for sure, information you type in manually is always better remembered than information which comes courtesy of someone else.

Keen is one of a number of successful stallions sired by Sharpen Up

Chapter 2

Sire, Dam and Damsire

The breeding of racehorses is not an exact science, which is just as well as racing depends, to a large extent, on the glorious uncertainty of it all. Yet breeders, owners and trainers are willing to spend millions of pounds each year on horses who are wholly unproven on the racetrack. Most place their faith in two things; the conformation of a horse, and its breeding.

Because Form Sires is a book about pedigree handicapping we can put aside the physicalities of the racehorse (Nick Mordin covers this angle anyway in his book 'The Winning Look') and concentrate on the three-generation pedigree of, for example, Blue Duster. I am not going to go into great detail at this stage, but I think it's important to show how a pedigree hangs together, and to familiarise ourselves with some of the terminology.

The SIRE (father) of Blue Duster is Danzig, the DAM (mother) is Blue Note, and the DAMSIRE (the father of the mother of Blue Duster) is Habitat. Danzig and Blue Note are found in the first generation of Blue Duster's pedigree.

Northern Dancer is Blue Duster's paternal grandsire, that is, he is the grandsire on the male side of the pedigree. Habitat is the maternal grandsire (also known as damsire) and is found on the female side of the pedigree. Both are found in the second generation of Blue Duster's pedigree.

Nearctic and Admirals Voyage are Blue Duster's paternal great-grandsires, while Sir Gaylord and Tourangeau are the maternal great-grandsires. They are found in the third generation of Blue Duster's pedigree.

Danzig, Northern Dancer and Nearctic form the dominant sire line within Blue Duster's pedigree.

Blue Note is the first dam in Blue Duster's pedigree, Balsamique is Blue Duster's second dam, and Bruyere is the third dam. This succession is often refered to as the female line.

Form Sires

Blue Duster

Danzig

Northern Dancer

Nearctic

Natalma

Pas De Nom

AdmiralsVoyage

Petitioner

Blue Note

Habitat

Sir Gaylord

Little Hut

Balsamique

Tourangeau

Bruyere

Form Sires

Sire

The sire can be responsible for many of the influences and traits handed down to its progeny. Not only has it proven itself to be superior to most other horses on the racetrack, it is usually the product of other highly regarded animals. This 'quality' of performance and breeding is what attracts owners of broodmares, and such sires are apt to be sent the very best.

Their future at stud then depends, to a large extent, on the racecourse performances of their first or second crops (A 'crop' is the total number of horses bred by a sire in a single season). If their early progeny show they are winners (especially at a higher level) then the sires responsible should continue to be popular with breeders. But should their progeny fail to shine at the racing game then breeders of the better broodmares may start to look elsewhere.

Many a 'disappointing' sire has been shipped off to ply his trade overseas, only for its future offspring to display the 'winability' and class that was missing from its earlier crops. It seems everyone wants success yesterday, and this fickleness within the breeding industry is one reason why some sires don't get the patronage they deserve. Just as every jockey needs to get on the best horses, so sires need to get on the best broodmares - literally!

Sires are the number one resource for the pedigree handicapper. The racing exploits of their progeny provide the crunchable data we need to determine which traits are being handed down from one generation to another.

Like humans, not all sires are equal. Some sires are more potent than others and will get more than their fair share of winners, with many of their offspring achieving success in Listed or Group-class races. Super sires, such as Nureyev and Danzig, breed into their stock a willingness to run, and a consistency of performance that puts the progeny of other sires to shame.

Dam

The dam of a successful racehorse may have been brilliant herself, or she may have been as slow as a donkey, or she may never have seen a racecourse. Either way, each type of dam (or broodmare) is capable of producing a top-class racehorse if its extended pedigree stands up to inspection.

Breeders will often look past the limited racecourse achievements of a broodmare if she has been responsible for previous winners - or if they believe abilities and qualities from its female ancestors may trickle through.

Form Sires

Unfortunately, broodmares are only able to produce one offspring per year, which is rather limiting from a PH point of view. PH needs plenty of statistical data if it is to have any real meaning, so we need to look elsewhere.

Damsire

The sire of a dam of a racehorse is known as the maternal grandsire - or damsire (or, if you live in America, broodmare sire). Potent damsires can be responsible for many winner-producing broodmares, and the racecourse performances of their collective offspring can be analysed and findings attributed to this one particular source.

A potent damsire will usually have a greater influence within the pedigree of a racehorse if the sire is markedly less potent, or if the female line is not a strong one. And my limited research suggests that sires who are more successful with their female offspring than their male, also make better damsires (probably because their influence is more easily transmitted through the female line).

Damsires make excellent vehicles for PH analysis. Most have a long history of producing winners, both as damsires, and as first-generation sires of yesteryear (if you can dig the info out). And the most potent of these are more than capable of passing on their influence to the progeny of their female offspring.

The Extended Pedigree

Sires and damsires form the foundations of pedigree handicapping, but it is always temping to want to examine their extended pedigrees in the hope of spotting a common sire from which the major traits are emerging.

At the back of this book there is an index to both sires and damsires, and part of the index has been sorted using either the sire's-sire or the damsire's-sire. The reason for this is simple. It allows us to see which sires or damsires have a common ancestry.

For example, Beveled, Diesis, Keen, Kris, Selkirk and Sharpo all have Sharpen Up as their common sire. If most favoured, say, soft ground, we could look to their common sire and see that he is a major influence for this particular trait.

Once we had in mind a list of common sires we would be able to look at the pedigrees of other horses with much more certainty. We would be able to name many common sires within a single pedigree, and give a pretty good account of the traits that were likely to emerge. Not only would this be a very satisfying thing to do (from a personal point of view), but it would encourage us to use this information with confidence - in the betting ring.

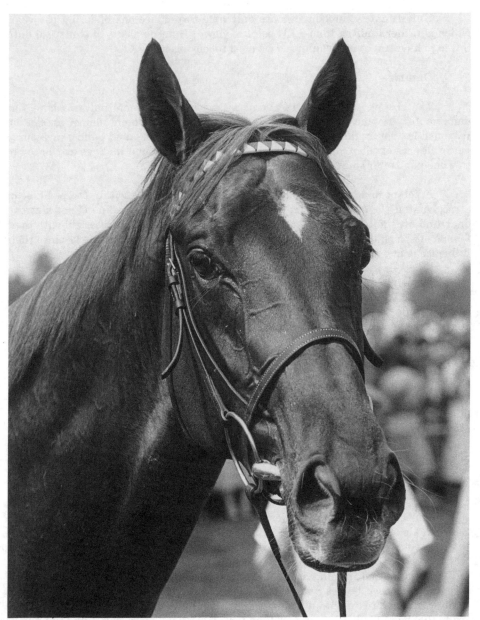

Derby winner Nashwan displays plenty of speed in his dosage profile

Chapter 3

The Major Form Factors

Most horseplayers know the value of form. They know the factors which are likely to come into play and affect the result of each race. Yet many are often frustrated because horses with short racing careers just do not carry with them the necessary data on which sound judgements can be made. This is especially true for two and three-year-olds, whose careers might consist of no more than half a dozen races.

Pedigree handicapping allows the horseplayer to make decisions about form based on the past exploits of a sire's progeny. This increased knowledge enables the player to weigh up the chances of every runner in the field, and so increase the opportunities to bet. How often have you left a race alone because you were not sure of the form of a lightly-raced favourite? This almost happened to me at an All-Weather meeting recently. I had a horse well clear on my figures and it was quoted at 9-2 in my racing paper. The 9-4 favourite had never run on the All-Weather but had good turf form. I needed some information about the favourite that would either make me fear it, or bet against it. I discovered a little later that its damsire, Mummy's Pet, had a terrible strike rate with his progeny on the AW (something like 4%), so there was a good chance the favourite would not take to the surface. This is exactly what happened. The horse never got going in the dirt and finished unplaced, while my selection ran a blinder - only to get beaten a head by one of the other runners!

I was also able to bet against Centre Stalls in the Wulfrun Stakes at Wolverhampton in December 1997. As you know, the horse is very classy, which made him red-hot favourite for the event, even though he had never raced on the All-Weather before. I did a bit of breeding analysis and found that his sire, In The Wings, has a strike rate of 15% with his progeny on turf, and a strike rate of only 9% when his runners tackled the dirt. This one factor alone made his odds look ridiculously small, and I was able to bet Farmost with confidence. Centre Stalls struggled all the way and finished last, while the less-classy Farmost was totally at home on the surface and ran out a ready winner at 7-1.

To make decisions like these the horseplayer needs data such as can be found in this book. It contains most of what is needed to make the connection between pedigree information and the major form factors.

Form Sires

Rate Of Maturity

Some sires and damsires are able to get progeny who are early-maturing sorts. These sharp juveniles are often able to dominate their generation and take most of the major prizes. It is well documented that breeders are going more for early speed (and the commercial benefits associated with it) than they are in producing stock which takes longer to mature. It is noticeable that top winning two-year-olds who disappoint at three are still in big demand when they go to stud. This is a trend that definitely needs to be reversed if we are not to end up with 'early' horses who have nowhere to go from the summer of their third year onwards. However, the economics of the situation seem to make this almost impossible. From a pedigree handicapping point of view I have produced performance tables which will feature those sires and damsires who are best at getting early sorts.

One of the ways to encourage breeders to produce horses with some sort of shelf-life, is to offer much increased prize money for horses who win prizes at three years of age - preferably by positioning the classics further towards the back end of the season. That way sharp two-year-olds, who manage to hang on to their abilities until the spring of their third year, would be burned out by the time the big money came up for grabs, and those who took the long view (breeding, owning and training wise) would get their rewards. I believe we are pushing our horses along too quickly, instead of letting them develop in a more natural way, which is why we don't often see the likes of a Pilsudski or Singspiel. From a pedigree handicapping point of view I have produced performance tables which will feature those sires and damsires who are best at getting horses of the 'Classic' generation.

I have also produced tables that show which sires' and damsires' progeny make the most improvement from two to three years of age. This arrangement penalises those who produce 'early sorts' and rewards those whose progeny score well at three. It is very noticeable that, on the sires improvement table for age (from two to three years), Mr Prospector is almost wiped out! Mr Prospector is very much an influence for precocity and speed, and while I believe he is a very classy sire, who gets very consistent performers, I can't help but think that the traits he is passing on are not the ones which will benefit the breeding industry in the long term. From a pedigree handicapping point of view these tables will help you to spot those sires and damsires whose stock should improve from the summer of their third year onwards.

Going Requirements

Phil Bull used to say that the going is the most important factor in determining the outcome of most races, and I do not think this theory has ever been disproved. It is vital that a horse can handle the underfoot conditions, if not it is likely to run many lengths below its best form. Form Sires will split the going into

Form Sires

two sections. The 'Firm Going' tables will show those sires whose progeny performed best on hard, firm and good-to-firm going, while the 'Soft Going' tables will show those sires whose progeny performed best on heavy, soft and good-to-soft going. I have found these tables to be especially useful when heavy rain arrives after a long dry spell and the going quickly changes from firm to soft. In these situations a soft-ground horse who has accumulated a row of duck eggs on the recent firm ground will suddenly find its form - and at very rewarding odds. It may never have raced on soft ground before, but if the progeny of its sire relishes such conditions then we will be aware of it.

Distance Requirements

Some horses are bred to be speedy two-year-olds, and will often run their rivals ragged over sprint distances (five and six furlongs), during the first half of the Flat season. Tables have been produced to show which sires and damsires are responsible for these whirlwinds on legs.

Other two-year-olds take more time to develop, but are still forward enough to compete as juveniles. Many are quickly stepped up to distances of seven or eight furlongs so as to avoid the 'speed' horses', and to make the most of any staying blood in their pedigrees. Tables have been produced to show which sires and damsires get early sorts who need a trip.

Horses stepping up to their 'correct' distance can improve dramatically on anything they have done before. Breeding can give us a good insight into the possibilities of such improvement and we can use this knowledge to our financial advantage. Form Sires, using data relating to horses aged three years and over, will split the distance requirements into four sections. The 'Sprint' table will show those sires whose progeny performed best at five and six furlongs. The 'Mile' table will show those sires whose progeny performed best at seven, eight and nine furlongs. The 'Middle' table will cover the distances ten to twelve furlongs, while the 'Long' table will cover the distances of thirteen furlongs and over.

Weight-Carrying Ability

Some racing pundits think the weight on a horse's back has no bearing on the result of a race, while others go the other way and over-compensate for any weight fluctuations that occur. Pedigree handicapping shows us that weight does matter - sometimes! That is, the progeny of some sires are able to carry weight more easily than others, and so any extra weight placed on their backs should have a limited

Form Sires

effect. Form Sires will identify those sires responsible for producing progeny that have the ability to carry weight.

Sires For The All-Weather

The progeny of some sires are strictly turf animals and can find themselves all at sea when asked to race on dirt tracks (such as Centre Stalls). Others show immediate improvement when switched from turf to dirt (such as Cigar, who, after a modest turf career, switched to dirt and became champion of America - and then world champion when winning in Dubai). Form Sires will identify those sires whose progeny either love or hate the dirt (or should that be 'ate' the dirt!).

Rest-Pattern

I don't know if Nick Mordin coined the phrase 'rest-pattern' but he says in his book 'Betting For A Living' that it describes horses having either their first run(s) of the season, or horses returning to the track having been rested for six weeks or more. I have always had plenty of time for this idea and you only have to watch racing regularly to see horses running above themselves when coming to their races 'fresh'. A good many horseplayers are suspicious of horses who have been off the track for some time, but for the progeny of some sires it is an added bonus.

Track Type

American courses are pretty uniform in their construction, and so, from a PH point of view, not much can be gained from a study of their characteristics. But here in the UK our racecourses come in all shapes and sizes, and these differences can either help or hinder the chances of those horses who compete on them. Form Sires will list those sires whose progeny perform well on either 'Stiff', 'Easy', 'Sharp', 'Galloping' or 'Undulating' tracks.

Sires Of Handicap Winners

The figures for some of our top stallions take a knock as we discover that handicaps help to even out the score between the progeny of the very best sires, and those of a less distinguished parentage. We will also discover which sires' progeny are most capable of increasing their tally by studying the 'winability' factor.

Form Sires

Chapter 4

The Performance Tables: Introduction

The performance tables are the life-blood of this book. Even if my ramblings get washed away with the passage of time I hope the hard facts and figures presented here will help you to a greater understanding of the sires and damsires associated with them. I would like to have produced information on every sire and damsire, and covered every possible form angle, but unfortunately space (and time) would not permit this. However, I have managed to include information on 150 of our top sires, as well as producing data for 106 of our best broodmare sires (damsires). This, I hope, will provide you plenty of punting ammunition as we apply the art and science of pedigree handicapping to the task of winner-finding.

Consistency Tables

SIRE - CONSISTENCY TABLE - SOFT

SIRE	SIRES' SIRE	WINS	RUNS	SR%
Mr Prospector	Raise A Native	10	37	27.03
Tragic Role	Nureyev	14	62	22.58
Polar Falcon	Nureyev	16	71	22.54
Sadler's Wells	Northern Dancer	101	463	21.81
Doyoun	Mill Reef	16	78	20.51
Zilzal	Nureyev	11	54	20.37
Danzig	Northern Dancer	19	95	20.00
El Gran Senor	Northern Dancer	19	96	19.79
Selkirk	Sharpen Up	11	57	19.30
Generous	Caerleon	21	110	19.09

Consistency tables are based on the strike rate achieved by the progeny of either the sire or damsire when testing for a particular trait. It is important to remember that some sires are good in almost every department, and that they can produce the goods (winners) at an alarmingly consistent rate. There is also a strong correlation between consistency and class, which seems to fall in line with the accepted wisdom that higher class animals are more genuine.

The consistency tables for both sires and damsires show the number of wins (**WINS**), to the number of runs (**RUNS**), of the progeny of each sire, together with the resulting strike rate in percentage terms (**SR%**). The top thirty sires or damsires in each category are listed according to their strike rate.

Form Sires

In the example above we can see the sires' names in bold, followed by the name of the sire's sire. We then have the three columns of information that give us the 'WINS', 'RUNS' and 'SR%'.

Improvement Tables

SIRE - IMPROVEMENT TABLE - SOFT

SIRE	SIRE'S SIRE	OSR	RULE	IMP
Tragic Role	Nureyev	12.89	22.58	1.75
Broken Hearted	Dara Monarch	11.63	17.91	1.54
Polar Falcon	Nureyev	15.14	22.54	1.49
Unfuwain	Northern Dancer	13.58	19.08	1.41
Bering	Arctic Tern	12.96	17.65	1.36
Risk Me	Sharpo	6.83	9.25	1.35
Riverman	Never Bend	10.63	14.12	1.33
Never So Bold	Bold Lad (IRE)	7.55	9.94	1.32
Nordico	Northern Dancer	9.81	12.64	1.29
Doyoun	Mill Reef	15.94	20.51	1.29

The improvement tables for both sires and damsires show the overall strike rate in percentage terms **(OSR%)**, the strike rate under rule **(RULE%)**, together with the improvement rating **(IMP)**.

The improvement rating is a figure which results from dividing the 'RULE%' by the 'OSR%'. So if the 'OSR' was 20% and the 'RULE' was 40% the improvement rating would be 2.00 (40 divided by 20 = 2), which tells us that the progeny of a particular sire won twice as often when under rule.

The word 'Rule' is used to describe the conditions under which we test for a particular trait. For example, we may wish to see which sires' progeny score most often when the going is soft. So we would tell the database to only search for races when the official going was soft. This would be a 'Rule' and the resulting strike rate (in percentage terms) would be associated with it.

Some Pedigree Handicappers prefer to use improvement tables, as they readily show any effect a trait is having on a sire's overall strike rate.

For example, Shareef Dancer has a rather lowly OSR of 6.17%, but when we add a weight rule (only consider progeny who carry 9-7 or more) the strike rate rises to an acceptable 12.38%, which shows that the progeny of Shareef Dancer score just over twice as often when asked to carry weight (12.38 divided by 6.17 = 2.01 rounded).

Which Performance Tables Are Best?

This improvement rating (2.01) would find Shareef Dancer a lofty position on an improvement table, but the 12.38% strike rate achieved when his progeny carried weight would not show on many consistency tables as it is still too low (most qualifiers muster a figure of 15% plus).

Conversely, a sire's progeny may score well when carrying weight (over 15%) yet still fail to find a place on an improvement table because its OSR is even higher! For example, Nureyev has an OSR of 22.57%, and this figure falls to 20.45% when its progeny are asked to carry weight, which means its improvement rating is only 0.91 (20.45 divided by 22.57 = 0.91 rounded).

It is clear that Nureyev's progeny perform slightly worse when asked to carry weight. So, does this mean Nureyev's progeny are inferior to those of Shareef Dancer in the weight-carrying department? The answer is no, because Nureyev's progeny recorded a strike rate of 20.45% when asked to carry weight, compared to a strike rate of 12.38% recorded by the offspring of Shareef Dancer.

What we can say is that the progeny of Shareef Dancer are likely to **show more improvement** when asked to carry weight than are the progeny of Nureyev, but that Nureyev's progeny are still likely to **win more consistently** when asked to carry the extra burden.

Both 'consistency' and 'improvement' tables are of equal importance to the pedigree handicapper. To display one without the other would only tell half the story.

The Sire Tables

The sire tables (consistency and improvement) have been compiled using *Computer Raceform*, and cover the last four Flat racing seasons (1994-1997 inclusive). Every effort has been made to ensure that the figures they contain are accurate, but with the many thousand key strokes needed for their compilation I am sure someone somewhere will find the odd blip!

The Damsire Tables

The damsire tables (consistency and improvement) have been compiled using Racing System Builder (RSB), and cover the last four Flat racing seasons up to 1996.

Form Sires

I was not able to include the 1997 Flat racing season data because it was not ready in time for inclusion in this book. However, most of the damsires have plenty of statistical data behind them, so their traits are more likely to be known than are those of younger sires. Many thanks to Tim Drakeford at RSB for letting me have the necessary software.

Derby winner Kahyasi is from the Northern Dancer sire line

Form Sires

Chapter 5

Performance Tables: Rate Of Maturity

SIRE - CONSISTENCY TABLE - AGE (2)

SIRE	SIRE'S SIRE	WINS	RUNS	SR%
Mr Prospector	Raise A Native	24	77	31.17
Nashwan	Blushing Groom	32	103	31.07
Dayjur	Danzig	32	108	29.63
Danzig	Northern Dancer	33	112	29.46
Great Commotion	Nureyev	10	38	26.32
Gone West	Mr Prospector	21	83	25.30
Machiavellian	Mr Prospector	25	99	25.25
El Gran Senor	Northern Dancer	25	106	23.58
Diesis	Sharpen Up	29	130	22.31
Groom Dancer	Blushing Groom	16	72	22.22
Nureyev	Northern Dancer	19	89	21.35
Generous	Caerleon	24	114	21.05
Sadler's Wells	Northern Dancer	38	181	20.99
Selkirk	Sharpen Up	22	108	20.37
Red Ransom	Roberto	18	90	20.00
Shavian	Kris	22	112	19.64
Warning	Known Fact	55	281	19.57
Fairy King	Northern Dancer	62	322	19.25
Doyoun	Mill Reef	13	69	18.84
Cadeaux Genereux	Young Generation	33	178	18.54
Irish River	Riverman	10	55	18.18
Silver Hawk	Roberto	15	83	18.07
Green Desert	Danzig	54	304	17.76
Zilzal	Nureyev	14	79	17.72
Polar Falcon	Nureyev	30	170	17.65
Royal Academy	Nijinsky	48	277	17.33
Danehill	Danzig	66	382	17.28
Lycius	Mr Prospector	30	174	17.24
Darshaan	Shirley Heights	13	76	17.11
Unfuwain	Northern Dancer	19	115	16.52

Form Sires

DAMSIRE - CONSISTENCY TABLE - AGE (2)

DAMSIRE	DAMSIRES' SIRE	WINS	RUNS	SR%
Exclusive Native	Raise A Native	12	46	26.09
Affirmed	Exclusive Native	13	54	24.07
Mr Prospector	Raise A Native	27	121	22.31
Dancing Brave	Lyphard	9	44	20.45
Lyphard	Northern Dancer	33	165	20.00
Rarity	Hethersett	13	66	19.70
Secreto	Northern Dancer	11	57	19.30
Rainbow Quest	Blushing Groom	11	58	18.97
Sadler's Wells	Northern Dancer	20	111	18.02
Shirley Heights	Mill Reef	44	246	17.89
Nureyev	Northern Dancer	24	139	17.27
Relkino	Relko	20	122	16.39
Arctic Tern	Sea-Bird II	24	148	16.22
Rousillon	Riverman	13	81	16.05
The Minstrel	Northern Dancer	30	187	16.04
Kris	Sharpen Up	40	251	15.94
Northern Dancer	Nearctic	17	109	15.60
Danzig	Northern Dancer	11	72	15.28
Irish River	Riverman	18	118	15.25
Mill Reef	Never Bend	33	217	15.21
Night Shift	Northern Dancer	9	60	15.00
Chief Singer	Ballad Rock	14	94	14.89
Nebbiolo	Yellow God	12	82	14.63
Habitat	Sir Gaylord	70	479	14.61
Secretariat	Bold Ruler	11	77	14.29
Riverman	Never Bend	23	161	14.29
Pharly	Lyphard	24	170	14.12
Try My Best	Northern Dancer	10	71	14.08
Alzao	Lyphard	22	157	14.01
Mummy's Pet	Sing Sing	71	512	13.87

Form Sires

SIRE - IMPROVEMENT TABLE - AGE (2)

SIRE	SIRE'S SIRE	OSR	RULE	IMP
Nashwan	Blushing Groom	16.31	31.07	1.90
Lycius	Mr Prospector	10.51	17.24	1.64
Irish River	Riverman	11.28	18.18	1.61
Great Commotion	Nureyev	16.38	26.32	1.61
Groom Dancer	Blushing Groom	13.84	22.22	1.61
Dayjur	Danzig	19.13	29.63	1.55
Shavian	Kris	12.79	19.64	1.54
El Gran Senor	Northern Dancer	15.40	23.58	1.53
Gone West	Mr Prospector	16.62	25.30	1.52
Thatching	Thatch	9.02	13.71	1.52
Tirol	Thatching	8.81	13.24	1.50
Diesis	Sharpen Up	15.05	22.31	1.48
Fairy King	Northern Dancer	13.13	19.25	1.47
Lugana Beach	Tumble Wind	10.51	15.38	1.46
Warning	Known Fact	13.47	19.57	1.45
Ballad Rock	Bold Lad (IRE)	6.98	10.06	1.44
Machiavellian	Mr Prospector	17.87	25.25	1.41
Mr Prospector	Raise A Native	22.30	31.17	1.40
Danzig	Northern Dancer	21.36	29.46	1.38
Nomination	Dominion	7.37	10.14	1.38
Prince Sabo	Young Generation	7.98	10.79	1.35
Primo Dominie	Dominion	9.58	12.95	1.35
Silver Hawk	Roberto	13.58	18.07	1.33
Slip Anchor	Shirley Heights	12.14	16.13	1.33
Green Desert	Danzig	13.48	17.76	1.32
Lahib	Riverman	11.50	15.00	1.30
Darshaan	Shirley Heights	13.24	17.11	1.29
Cadeaux Genereux	Young Generation	14.38	18.54	1.29
Mujtahid	Woodman	11.09	14.29	1.29
Waajib	Try My Best	8.31	10.70	1.29

Form Sires

DAMSIRE	DAMSIRE'S SIRE	OSR	RULE	IMP
Mr Prospector	Raise A Native	12.94	22.31	1.72
Mummy's Pet	Sing Sing	8.06	13.87	1.72
Relkino	Relko	9.64	16.39	1.70
Ballad Rock	Bold Lad (IRE)	7.79	13.19	1.69
Try My Best	Northern Dancer	8.38	14.08	1.68
Affirmed	Exclusive Native	14.81	24.07	1.63
Nureyev	Northern Dancer	11.52	17.27	1.50
Lyphard	Northern Dancer	13.68	20.00	1.46
Rarity	Hethersett	13.71	19.70	1.44
The Minstrel	Northern Dancer	11.37	16.04	1.41
Kris	Sharpen Up	11.52	15.94	1.38
Shirley Heights	Mill Reef	12.97	17.89	1.38
Main Reef	Mill Reef	8.48	11.61	1.37
Welsh Pageant	Tudor Melody	10.19	13.55	1.33
Rainbow Quest	Blushing Groom	14.40	18.97	1.32
Lomond	Northern Dancer	9.80	12.80	1.31
Secretariat	Bold Ruler	11.31	14.61	1.29
Alzao	Lyphard	11.07	14.01	1.27
Dance In Time	Northern Dancer	10.86	13.71	1.26
Auction Ring	Bold Bidder	8.54	10.58	1.24
Nebbiolo	Yellow God	11.92	14.63	1.23
Exclusive Native	Raise A Native	21.30	26.09	1.22
Pharly	Lyphard	11.58	14.12	1.22
Chief Singer	Ballad Rock	12.27	14.89	1.21
Thatching	Thatch	9.96	11.95	1.20
Ela-Mana-Mou	Pitcairn	10.50	12.59	1.20
Secreto	Northern Dancer	16.13	19.30	1.20
Bay Express	Polyfoto	9.24	10.95	1.18
Runnett	Mummy's Pet	7.73	9.04	1.17

Form Sires

SIRE - CONSISTENCY TABLE - AGE (3)

SIRE	SIRE'S SIRE	WINS	RUNS	SR%
Nureyev	Northern Dancer	49	213	23.00
Storm Cat	Storm Bird	17	81	20.99
Manila	Lyphard	10	48	20.83
Alleged	Hoist The Flag	34	169	20.12
Sadler's Wells	Northern Dancer	170	856	19.86
Generous	Caerleon	50	254	19.69
Mr Prospector	Raise A Native	33	176	18.75
Dixieland Band	Northern Dancer	15	81	18.52
Caerleon	Nijinsky	83	463	17.93
Rainbow Quest	Blushing Groom	66	374	17.65
Ela-Mana-Mou	Pitcairn	31	177	17.51
Kahyasi	Ile De Bourbon	22	126	17.46
Danzig	Northern Dancer	32	184	17.39
El Gran Senor	Northern Dancer	41	239	17.15
Selkirk	Sharpen Up	22	131	16.79
Silver Hawk	Roberto	34	205	16.59
Red Ransom	Roberto	14	85	16.47
Green Dancer	Nijinsky	21	128	16.41
Darshaan	Shirley Heights	45	276	16.30
Zilzal	Nureyev	36	222	16.22
Machiavellian	Mr Prospector	37	230	16.09
Rousillon	Riverman	14	88	15.91
Most Welcome	Be My Guest	75	483	15.53
Soviet Star	Nureyev	53	342	15.50
Doyoun	Mill Reef	23	150	15.33
Riverman	Never Bend	30	197	15.23
Danehill	Danzig	102	676	15.09
Dowsing	Riverman	56	372	15.05
Mtoto	Busted	62	416	14.90
In The Wings	Sadler's Wells	68	465	14.62

Form Sires

DAMSIRE - CONSISTENCY TABLE - AGE (3)

DAMSIRE	DAMSIRE'S SIRE	WINS	RUNS	SR%
Mount Hagen	Bold Bidder	24	92	26.09
Teenoso	Youth	10	40	25.00
Exclusive Native	Raise A Native	21	96	21.88
Topsider	Northern Dancer	24	113	21.24
Northern Dancer	Nearctic	57	277	20.58
Mill Reef	Never Bend	95	506	18.77
Dancing Brave	Lyphard	10	54	18.52
Arctic Tern	Sea-Bird II	33	179	18.44
Rousillon	Riverman	9	49	18.37
Caro	Fortino II	30	171	17.54
Night Shift	Northern Dancer	11	63	17.46
Frimley Park	Tribal Chief	11	67	16.42
Roberto	Hail To Reason	40	246	16.26
Key To The Mint	Graustark	10	62	16.13
Majestic Light	Majestic Prince	8	50	16.00
Shareef Dancer	Northern Dancer	41	263	15.59
Danzig	Northern Dancer	14	91	15.38
Secreto	Northern Dancer	14	91	15.38
Seattle Slew	Bold Reasoning	17	111	15.32
Riverman	Never Bend	42	275	15.27
Nijinsky	Northern Dancer	42	279	15.05
Affirmed	Exclusive Native	20	134	14.93
Kris	Sharpen Up	65	462	14.07
Troy	Petingo	36	257	14.01
Blushing Groom	Red God	47	355	13.24
Shirley Heights	Mill Reef	66	500	13.20
Fappiano	Mr Prospector	10	78	12.82
Be My Guest	Northern Dancer	69	544	12.68
High Top	Derring-Do	82	653	12.56
Irish River	Riverman	25	200	12.50

Form Sires

SIRE - IMPROVEMENT TABLE - AGE (3)

SIRE	SIRE'S SIRE	OSR	RULE	IMP
Mystiko	Secreto	6.97	11.90	1.71
Kahyasi	Ile De Bourbon	11.26	17.46	1.55
Shalford	Thatching	7.58	11.36	1.50
Riverman	Never Bend	10.63	15.23	1.43
Dowsing	Riverman	11.86	15.05	1.27
Persian Bold	Bold Lad (IRE)	11.43	14.43	1.26
Manila	Lyphard	16.56	20.83	1.26
Bluebird	Storm Bird	11.41	14.14	1.24
Rousillon	Riverman	12.85	15.91	1.24
Darshaan	Shirley Heights	13.24	16.30	1.23
Keen	Sharpen Up	7.53	9.27	1.23
Broken Hearted	Dara Monarch	11.63	14.29	1.23
Silver Hawk	Roberto	13.58	16.59	1.22
Most Welcome	Be My Guest	12.88	15.53	1.21
Red Sunset	Red God	9.48	11.40	1.20
Common Grounds	Kris	9.01	10.82	1.20
Kris	Sharpen Up	11.83	14.11	1.19
Warrshan	Northern Dancer	8.18	9.73	1.19
Rainbow Quest	Blushing Groom	15.02	17.65	1.17
Storm Cat	Storm Bird	17.96	20.99	1.17
Dixieland Band	Northern Dancer	15.95	18.52	1.16
Mtoto	Busted	12.92	14.90	1.15
Clantime	Music Boy	9.30	10.71	1.15
Rock City	Ballad Rock	9.77	11.23	1.15
Robellino	Roberto	10.30	11.83	1.15
Alzao	Lyphard	12.23	14.04	1.15
Alleged	Hoist The Flag	17.86	20.12	1.13
Caerleon	Nijinsky	15.97	17.93	1.12
Roi Danzig	Danzig	10.62	11.88	1.12
Damister	Mr Prospector	10.09	11.26	1.12

Form Sires

DAMSIRE	DAMSIRE'S SIRE	OSR	RULE	IMP
Mount Hagen	Bold Bidder	16.84	26.09	1.55
Frimley Park	Tribal Chief	11.27	16.42	1.46
Caro	Fortino II	12.62	17.54	1.39
Northern Dancer	Nearctic	15.30	20.58	1.34
Niniski	Nijinsky	9.13	12.24	1.34
Sir Ivor	Sir Gaylord	8.89	11.87	1.34
Arctic Tern	Sea-Bird II	14.04	18.44	1.31
Great Nephew	Honeyway	8.74	11.22	1.28
Auction Ring	Bold Bidder	8.54	10.81	1.27
Kings Lake	Nijinsky	9.40	11.81	1.26
Alleged	Hoist The Flag	9.45	11.79	1.25
Topsider	Northern Dancer	17.21	21.24	1.23
Kris	Sharpen Up	11.52	14.07	1.22
Seattle Slew	Bold Reasoning	12.57	15.32	1.22
Troy	Petingo	11.56	14.01	1.21
Grundy	Great Nephew	8.96	10.84	1.21
Night Shift	Northern Dancer	14.72	17.46	1.19
Godswalk	Dancer's Image	8.45	10.00	1.18
Blakeney	Hethersett	8.13	9.59	1.18
Welsh Saint	Sir Paddy	7.89	9.30	1.18
Key To The Mint	Graustark	13.74	16.13	1.17
Rousillon	Riverman	15.83	18.37	1.16
Busted	Crepello	10.74	12.43	1.16
Known Fact	In Reality	10.56	12.21	1.16
Runnett	Mummy's Pet	7.73	8.92	1.15
Mill Reef	Never Bend	16.29	18.77	1.15
Storm Bird	Northern Dancer	10.32	11.82	1.15
Be My Guest	Northern Dancer	11.16	12.68	1.14
Riverman	Never Bend	13.44	15.27	1.14
Shareef Dancer	Northern Dancer	13.72	15.59	1.14

Form Sires

SIRE - IMPROVEMENT TABLE - AGE (from 2 to 3 years)

SIRE	SIRE'S SIRE	2YO	3YO	IMP
Mystiko	Secreto	1.69	11.90	7.02
Bairn	Northern Baby	1.79	6.77	3.79
Old Vic	Sadler's Wells	3.92	13.09	3.34
Pennine Walk	Persian Bold	2.56	6.56	2.56
Broken Hearted	Dara Monarch	6.25	14.29	2.29
Alleged	Hoist The Flag	11.76	20.12	1.71
Be My Guest	Northern Dancer	6.62	11.31	1.71
Never So Bold	Bold Lad (IRE)	4.93	8.38	1.70
Persian Bold	Bold Lad (IRE)	8.81	14.43	1.64
Most Welcome	Be My Guest	9.55	15.53	1.63
Clantime	Music Boy	6.59	10.71	1.63
Safawan	Young Generation	6.49	10.45	1.61
Bluebird	Storm Bird	8.97	14.14	1.58
Kefaah	Blushing Groom	6.25	9.57	1.53
Dominion	Derring-Do	6.76	10.29	1.52
Green Dancer	Nijinsky	11.11	16.41	1.48
Keen	Sharpen Up	6.59	9.27	1.41
Soviet Star	Nureyev	11.11	15.50	1.39
Nordico	Northern Dancer	7.80	10.83	1.39
Damister	Mr Prospector	8.14	11.26	1.38
Red Sunset	Red God	8.28	11.40	1.38
Kahyasi	Ile De Bourbon	13.04	17.46	1.34
Petoski	Niniski	7.27	9.36	1.29
Warrshan	Northern Dancer	7.75	9.73	1.26
Saddlers' Hall	Sadler's Wells	8.86	11.11	1.25
Sharrood	Caro	10.23	12.73	1.25
In The Wings	Sadler's Wells	11.90	14.62	1.23
Priolo	Sovereign Dancer	11.11	13.64	1.23
Rock City	Ballad Rock	9.18	11.23	1.22
Cyrano De Bergerac	Bold Lad (IRE)	6.30	7.60	1.21
Robellino	Roberto	9.82	11.83	1.20

Form Sires

DAMSIRE	DAMSIRE'S SIRE	2YO	3YO	IMP
Troy	Petingo	4.76	14.01	2.94
Caro	Fortino II	6.15	17.54	2.85
Alleged	Hoist The Flag	4.76	11.79	2.48
Great Nephew	Honeyway	4.71	11.22	2.38
Reform	Pall Mall	3.96	8.59	2.17
Sir Ivor	Sir Gaylord	6.87	11.87	1.73
Blakeney	Hethersett	6.10	9.59	1.57
Formidable	Forli	6.13	9.49	1.55
Teenoso	Youth	16.67	25.00	1.50
Godswalk	Dancer's Image	7.06	10.00	1.42
Kings Lake	Nijinsky	8.55	11.81	1.38
Habat	Habitat	5.66	7.69	1.36
Mount Hagen	Bold Bidder	19.35	26.09	1.35
Busted	Crepello	9.35	12.43	1.33
Northern Dancer	Nearctic	15.60	20.58	1.32
Topsider	Northern Dancer	16.33	21.24	1.30
Frimley Park	Tribal Chief	12.73	16.42	1.29
Roberto	Hail To Reason	12.68	16.26	1.28
Grundy	Great Nephew	8.52	10.84	1.27
Ile De Bourbon	Nijinsky	9.24	11.62	1.26
General Assembly	Secretariat	7.32	9.09	1.24
Niniski	Never Bend	15.21	18.77	1.23
Halo	Kalamoun	9.92	12.23	1.23
Be My Guest	Northern Dancer	10.33	12.68	1.23
Indian King	Raja Baba	9.69	11.61	1.20
Shareef Dancer	Northern Dancer	13.21	15.59	1.18
Night Shift	Northern Dancer	15.00	17.46	1.16
High Line	High Hat	9.52	11.00	1.16

Form Sires

Chapter 6

Performance Tables: Going requirements

SIRE - CONSISTENCY TABLE - FIRM

SIRE	SIRE'S SIRE	WINS	RUNS	SR%
Nureyev	Northern Dancer	44	187	23.53
Dayjur	Danzig	28	128	21.88
Mr Prospector	Raise A Native	28	130	21.54
Dixieland Band	Northern Dancer	20	96	20.83
Danzig	Northern Dancer	39	192	20.31
Green Dancer	Nijinsky	18	89	20.22
Red Ransom	Roberto	16	81	19.75
Generous	Caerleon	31	158	19.62
Gone West	Mr Prospector	32	165	19.39
Caerleon	Nijinsky	74	395	18.73
Storm Cat	Storm Bird	19	102	18.63
Manila	Lyphard	10	54	18.52
Nashwan	Blushing Groom	43	247	17.41
In The Wings	Sadler's Wells	25	144	17.36
Sadler's Wells	Northern Dancer	91	526	17.30
Mtoto	Busted	61	354	17.23
Diesis	Sharpen Up	50	293	17.06
Groom Dancer	Blushing Groom	22	134	16.42
Alleged	Hoist The Flag	24	147	16.33
Zilzal	Nureyev	30	187	16.04
Cadeaux Genereux	Young Generation	83	519	15.99
Known Fact	In Reality	20	126	15.87
Green Desert	Danzig	110	699	15.74
Danehill	Danzig	92	587	15.67
Ela-Mana-Mou	Pitcairn	33	213	15.49
Warning	Known Fact	82	533	15.38
Rainbow Quest	Blushing Groom	60	391	15.35
Rousillon	Riverman	31	204	15.20
Soviet Star	Nureyev	44	292	15.07
Selkirk	Sharpen Up	14	93	15.05

Form Sires

DAMSIRE	DAMSIRE'S SIRE	WINS	RUNS	SR%
Teenoso	Youth	10	38	26.32
Exclusive Native	Raise A Native	16	70	22.86
Dancing Brave	Lyphard	11	51	21.57
Fappiano	Mr Prospector	12	56	21.43
Mount Hagen	Bold Bidder	31	161	19.25
Topsider	Northern Dancer	18	103	17.48
Mill Reef	Never Bend	90	518	17.37
Roberto	Hail To Reason	47	273	17.22
Arctic Tern	Sea-Bird II	39	229	17.03
Lyphard	Northern Dancer	53	312	16.99
Vice Regent	Northern Dancer	11	66	16.67
Sadler's Wells	Northern Dancer	24	144	16.67
Kalaglow	Kalamoun	28	171	16.37
Nijinsky	Northern Dancer	62	393	15.78
Affirmed	Exclusive Native	17	108	15.74
Night Shift	Northern Dancer	11	70	15.71
Caro	Fortino II	43	277	15.52
Storm Bird	Northern Dancer	20	134	14.93
Rainbow Quest	Blushing Groom	10	67	14.93
Secreto	Northern Dancer	14	94	14.89
Seattle Slew	Bold Reasoning	25	168	14.88
Danzig	Northern Dancer	18	121	14.88
Frimley Park	Tribal Chief	18	123	14.63
Blushing Groom	Red God	58	403	14.39
Northern Dancer	Nearctic	42	292	14.38
Troy	Petingo	46	321	14.33
Riverman	Never Bend	49	342	14.33
Kris	Sharpen Up	69	485	14.23
Shareef Dancer	Northern Dancer	40	285	14.04
Shirley Heights	Mill Reef	75	539	13.91

Form Sires

SIRE	SIRE'S SIRE	OSR	RULE	IMP
Tirol	Thatching	8.81	12.11	1.37
Imp Society	Barrera	8.91	12.06	1.35
Green Dancer	Nijinsky	15.06	20.22	1.34
Mtoto	Busted	12.92	17.23	1.33
Persian Bold	Bold Lad (IRE)	11.43	15.00	1.31
Dixieland Band	Northern Dancer	15.95	20.83	1.31
Sayf El Arab	Drone	11.37	14.79	1.30
Great Commotion	Nureyev	16.38	21.21	1.30
Clantime	Music Boy	9.30	11.98	1.29
Puissance	Thatching	8.45	10.84	1.28
Ballad Rock	Bold Lad (IRE)	6.98	8.88	1.27
Nomination	Dominion	7.37	9.35	1.27
Archway	Thatching	8.43	10.58	1.25
Irish River	Riverman	11.28	14.12	1.25
Safawan	Young Generation	9.70	12.12	1.25
Rudimentary	Nureyev	7.55	9.40	1.25
Known Fact	In Reality	12.80	15.87	1.24
Never So Bold	Bold Lad (IRE)	7.55	9.20	1.22
Roi Danzig	Danzig	10.62	12.88	1.21
Mujtahid	Woodman	11.09	13.44	1.21
Treasure Kay	Mummy's Pet	9.55	11.54	1.21
Distinctly North	Minshaanshu Amad	9.34	11.14	1.19
Kefaah	Blushing Groom	10.86	12.94	1.19
In The Wings	Sadler's Wells	14.62	17.36	1.19
Groom Dancer	Blushing Groom	13.84	16.42	1.19
Rousillon	Riverman	12.85	15.20	1.18
Kahyasi	Ile De Bourbon	11.26	13.28	1.18
Salt Dome	Blushing Groom	7.76	9.15	1.18
Caerleon	Nijinsky	15.97	18.73	1.17
Reprimand	Mummy's Pet	9.14	10.71	1.17

Form Sires

DAMSIRE - IMPROVEMENT TABLE - FIRM

DAMSIRE	DAMSIRE'S SIRE	OSR	RULE	IMP
Fappiano	Mr Prospector	14.49	21.43	1.48
Storm Bird	Northern Dancer	10.32	14.93	1.45
Ballad Rock	Bold Lad (IRE)	7.79	11.18	1.44
Kings Lake	Nijinsky	9.40	13.45	1.43
Kalaglow	Kalamoun	12.54	16.37	1.31
Try My Best	Northern Dancer	8.38	10.92	1.30
Vice Regent	Northern Dancer	12.80	16.67	1.30
Habat	Habitat	8.44	10.98	1.30
Frimley Park	Tribal Chief	11.27	14.63	1.30
Main Reef	Mill Reef	8.48	10.83	1.28
Blakeney	Hethersett	8.13	10.37	1.28
Welsh Saint	St Paddy	7.89	9.87	1.25
Alzao	Lyphard	11.07	13.75	1.24
Lyphard	Northern Dancer	13.68	16.99	1.24
Troy	Petingo	11.56	14.33	1.24
Kris	Sharpen Up	11.52	14.23	1.23
Lord Gayle	Sir Gaylord	7.68	9.45	1.23
Caro	Fortino II	12.62	15.52	1.23
Persian Bold	Bold Lad (IRE)	10.93	13.39	1.23
Vaguely Noble	Vienna	11.17	13.62	1.22
Arctic Tern	Sea-Bird II	14.04	17.03	1.21
Bay Express	Polyfoto	9.24	11.01	1.19
Song	Sing Sing	8.91	10.61	1.19
Roberto	Hail To Reason	14.50	17.22	1.19
Bustino	Busted	9.06	10.74	1.19
Luthier	Klairon	11.11	13.16	1.18
Seattle Slew	Bold Reasoning	12.57	14.88	1.18
Pharly	Lyphard	11.58	13.61	1.17
Sir Ivor	Sir Gaylord	8.89	10.43	1.17
Blushing Groom	Red God	12.30	14.39	1.17

Form Sires

SIRE - CONSISTENCY TABLE - SOFT

SIRE	SIRE'S SIRE	WINS	RUNS	SR%
Mr Prospector	Raise A Native	10	37	27.03
Tragic Role	Nureyev	14	62	22.58
Polar Falcon	Nureyev	16	71	22.54
Sadler's Wells	Northern Dancer	101	463	21.81
Doyoun	Mill Reef	16	78	20.51
Zilzal	Nureyev	11	54	20.37
Danzig	Northern Dancer	19	95	20.00
El Gran Senor	Northern Dancer	19	96	19.79
Selkirk	Sharpen Up	11	57	19.30
Generous	Caerleon	21	110	19.09
Unfuwain	Northern Dancer	25	131	19.08
Alleged	Hoist The Flag	22	121	18.18
Machiavellian	Mr Prospector	16	89	17.98
Broken Hearted	Dara Monarch	12	67	17.91
Bering	Arctic Tern	18	102	17.65
Nureyev	Northern Dancer	18	103	17.48
Nashwan	Blushing Groom	18	108	16.67
Ela-Mana-Mou	Pitcairn	21	127	16.54
Cadeaux Genereux	Young Generation	36	219	16.44
Fairy King	Northern Dancer	55	339	16.22
Diesis	Sharpen Up	21	132	15.91
Woodman	Mr Prospector	23	153	15.03
Slip Anchor	Shirley Heights	26	173	15.03
Danehill	Danzig	50	342	14.62
Sharrood	Caro	13	89	14.61
Shaadi	Danzig	15	104	14.42
Darshaan	Shirley Heights	21	146	14.38
Riverman	Never Bend	12	85	14.12
In The Wings	Sadler's Wells	19	139	13.67
Old Vic	Sadler's Wells	13	97	13.40

Form Sires

DAMSIRE - CONSISTENCY TABLE - SOFT

DAMSIRE	DAMSIRE'S SIRE	WINS	RUNS	SR%
Northern Dancer	Nearctic	10	37	27.03
Affirmed	Exclusive Native	14	62	22.58
Mr Prospector	Raise A Native	16	71	22.54
Shareef Dancer	Northern Dancer	101	463	21.81
Irish River	Riverman	16	78	20.51
Mill Reef	Never Bend	11	54	20.37
Riverman	Never Bend	19	95	20.00
Arctic Tern	Sea-Bird II	19	96	19.79
Hotfoot	Firestreak	11	57	19.30
Green Dancer	Nijinsky	21	110	19.09
Be My Guest	Northern Dancer	25	131	19.08
Thatching	Thatch	22	121	18.18
High Line	High Hat	16	89	17.98
Known Fact	In Reality	12	67	17.91
Mummy's Pet	Sing Sing	18	102	17.65
The Minstrel	Northern Dancer	18	103	17.48
Pas De Seul	Mill Reef	18	108	16.67
Lochnager	Dumbarnie	21	127	16.54
Ela-Mana-Mou	Pitcairn	36	219	16.44
Alleged	Hoist The Flag	55	339	16.22
Welsh Pageant	Tudor Melody	21	132	15.91
Dominion	Derring-Do	23	153	15.03
High Top	Derring-Do	26	173	15.03
Blushing Groom	Red God	50	342	14.62
Habitat	Sir Gaylord	13	89	14.61
Star Appeal	Appiani II	15	104	14.42
Northfields	Northern Dancer	21	146	14.38
Music Boy	Jukebox	12	85	14.12
Dance In Time	Northern Dancer	19	139	13.67
Busted	Crepello	13	97	13.40

Form Sires

SIRE - IMPROVEMENT TABLE - SOFT

SIRE	SIRE'S SIRE	OSR	RULE	IMP
Tragic Role	Nureyev	12.89	22.58	1.75
Broken Hearted	Dara Monarch	11.63	17.91	1.54
Polar Falcon	Nureyev	15.14	22.54	1.49
Unfuwain	Northern Dancer	13.58	19.08	1.41
Bering	Arctic Tern	12.96	17.65	1.36
Risk Me	Sharpo	6.83	9.25	1.35
Riverman	Never Bend	10.63	14.12	1.33
Never So Bold	Bold Lad (IRE)	7.55	9.94	1.32
Nordico	Northern Dancer	9.81	12.64	1.29
Doyoun	Mill Reef	15.94	20.51	1.29
El Gran Senor	Northern Dancer	15.40	19.79	1.29
Zilzal	Nureyev	16.40	20.37	1.24
Slip Anchor	Shirley Heights	12.14	15.03	1.24
Prince Sabo	Young Generation	7.98	9.88	1.24
Fairy King	Northern Dancer	13.13	16.22	1.24
Dominion	Derring-Do	10.07	12.44	1.24
Mr Prospector	Raise A Native	22.30	27.03	1.21
Sharrood	Caro	12.06	14.61	1.21
Red Sunset	Red God	9.48	11.21	1.18
Efisio	Formidable	11.11	13.07	1.18
Sadler's Wells	Northern Dancer	18.66	21.81	1.17
Beveled	Sharpen Up	9.60	11.21	1.17
Damister	Mr Prospector	10.09	11.76	1.17
Cadeaux Genereux	Young Generation	14.38	16.44	1.14
Old Vic	Sadler's Wells	11.74	13.40	1.14
Indian Ridge	Ahonoora	11.60	12.93	1.11
Distant Relative	Habitat	11.68	13.00	1.11
Kris	Sharpen Up	11.83	13.10	1.11
Marju	Last Tycoon	11.58	12.75	1.10
Don't Forget Me	Ahonoora	7.41	8.14	1.10

Form Sires

DAMSIRE	DAMSIRE'S SIRE	OSR	RULE	IMP
Mummy's Pet	Sing Sing	8.06	12.94	1.61
Mr Prospector	Raise A Native	12.94	17.58	1.36
Thatching	Thatch	9.96	13.46	1.35
Northern Dancer	Nearctic	15.30	19.54	1.28
Known Fact	In Reality	10.56	13.00	1.23
Hotfoot	Firestreak	11.84	14.55	1.23
Affirmed	Exclusive Native	14.81	18.18	1.23
Alleged	Hoist The Flag	9.45	11.58	1.23
Be My Guest	Northern Dancer	11.16	13.64	1.22
Irish River	Riverman	13.27	16.09	1.21
Shareef Dancer	Northern Dancer	13.72	16.44	1.20
Green Dancer	Nijinsky	12.00	14.13	1.18
Blakeney	Hethersett	8.13	9.54	1.17
Auction Ring	Bold Bidder	8.54	9.94	1.16
Lochnager	Dumbarnie	10.43	12.05	1.16
Star Appeal	Appiani II	9.44	10.83	1.15
The Minstrel	Northern Dancer	11.37	12.93	1.14
Welsh Pageant	Tudor Melody	10.19	11.54	1.13
Dominion	Derring-Do	10.09	11.24	1.11
Riverman	Never Bend	13.44	14.86	1.11
Ela-Mana-Mou	Pitcairn	10.50	11.61	1.11
Lord Gayle	Sir Gaylord	7.68	8.47	1.10
Pas De Seul	Mill Reef	11.51	12.61	1.10
High Line	High Hat	12.07	13.17	1.09
Music Boy	Jukebox	9.82	10.57	1.08
Arctic Tern	Sea-Bird II	14.04	14.86	1.06
Bay Express	Polyfoto	9.24	9.71	1.05
Godswalk	Dancer's Image	8.45	8.78	1.04
Northfields	Northern Dancer	10.93	10.82	0.99
Grundy	Great Nephew	8.96	8.77	0.98

Form Sires

Chapter 7

Performance Tables: Distance

SIRE - CONSISTENCY TABLE - SPRINT (2 y-o)

SIRE	SIRES-SIRE	WINS	RUNS	SR%
Dayjur	Danzig	30	87	34.48
Mr Prospector	Raise A Native	16	48	33.33
Gone West	Mr Prospector	13	40	32.50
Danzig	Northern Dancer	23	74	31.08
Red Ransom	Roberto	10	34	29.41
Lycius	Mr Prospector	21	81	25.93
Machiavellian	Mr Prospector	10	40	25.00
Shavian	Kris	18	75	24.00
Warning	Known Fact	33	148	22.30
Diesis	Sharpen Up	12	54	22.22
Cadeaux Genereux	Young Generation	20	92	21.74
Green Desert	Danzig	34	162	20.99
Nureyev	Northern Dancer	8	39	20.51
Lahib	Riverman	9	45	20.00
Zilzal	Nureyev	6	30	20.00
Danehill	Danzig	9	46	19.57
Fairy King	Northern Dancer	40	209	19.14
Dowsing	Riverman	19	103	18.45
Polar Falcon	Nureyev	16	89	17.98
Woodman	Mr Prospector	12	68	17.65
Selkirk	Sharpen Up	8	46	17.39
Lugana Beach	Tumble Wind	18	108	16.67
Mujtahid	Woodman	23	139	16.55
Indian Ridge	Ahonoora	27	164	16.46
El Gran Senor	Northern Dancer	6	37	16.22
Kris	Sharpen Up	6	37	16.22
Irish River	Riverman	5	31	16.13
Royal Academy	Nijinsky	18	112	16.07
Tirol	Thatching	16	102	15.69

Form Sires

DAMSIRE	DAMSIRE'S SIRE	WINS	RUNS	SR%
Rainbow Quest	Blushing Groom	10	34	29.41
Mr Prospector	Raise A Native	16	57	28.07
Lyphard	Northern Dancer	21	78	26.92
Rarity	Hethersett	12	50	24.00
Arctic Tern	Sea-Bird II	18	84	21.43
Seattle Slew	Bold Reasoning	6	29	20.69
Northern Dancer	Nearctic	11	55	20.00
The Minstrel	Northern Dancer	18	92	19.57
Relkino	Relko	15	77	19.48
Try My Best	Northern Dancer	9	49	18.37
Mill Reef	Never Bend	14	77	18.18
Bellypha	Lyphard	11	64	17.19
Artaius	Round Table	14	82	17.07
Kris	Sharpen Up	18	107	16.82
Night Shift	Northern Dancer	7	42	16.67
Sadler's Wells	Northern Dancer	6	36	16.67
Pharly	Lyphard	16	98	16.33
Alzao	Lyphard	12	74	16.22
Nureyev	Northern Dancer	11	69	15.94
Dance In Time	Northern Dancer	14	88	15.91
Ela-Mana-Mou	Pitcairn	11	71	15.49
Habitat	Sir Gaylord	41	271	15.13
Rousillon	Riverman	8	53	15.09
Shareef Dancer	Northern Dancer	19	126	15.08
Chief Singer	Ballad Rock	9	60	15.00
Red Alert	Red God	10	67	14.93
Mummy's Pet	Sing Sing	55	373	14.75
Ballad Rock	Bold Lad (IRE)	13	89	14.61
Diesis	Sharpen Up	8	55	14.55
Frimley Park	Tribal Chief	7	49	14.29

Form Sires

SIRE - IMPROVEMENT TABLE - SPRINT (2 y-o)

SIRE	SIRE'S SIRE	OSR	RULE	IMP
Lycius	Mr Prospector	10.51	25.93	2.47
Gone West	Mr Prospector	16.62	32.50	1.96
Shavian	Kris	12.79	24.00	1.88
Dayjur	Danzig	19.13	34.48	1.80
Tirol	Thatching	8.81	15.69	1.78
Lahib	Riverman	11.50	20.00	1.74
Rudimentary	Nureyev	7.55	13.10	1.73
Thatching	Thatch	9.02	15.45	1.71
Nomination	Dominion	7.37	12.37	1.68
Warning	Known Fact	13.47	22.30	1.66
Red Ransom	Roberto	18.28	29.41	1.61
Be My Chief	Chief's Crown	9.80	15.63	1.59
Lugana Beach	Tumble Wind	10.51	16.67	1.59
Waajib	Try My Best	8.31	13.16	1.58
Primo Dominie	Dominion	9.58	15.05	1.57
Green Desert	Danzig	13.48	20.99	1.56
Dowsing	Riverman	11.86	18.45	1.56
Cadeaux Genereux	Young Generation	14.38	21.74	1.51
Mr Prospector	Raise A Native	22.30	33.33	1.49
Mujtahid	Woodman	11.09	16.55	1.49
Diesis	Sharpen Up	15.05	22.22	1.48
Fairy King	Northern Dancer	13.13	19.14	1.46
Danzig	Northern Dancer	21.36	31.08	1.46
Emarati	Danzig	9.51	13.70	1.44
Irish River	Riverman	11.28	16.13	1.43
Indian Ridge	Ahonoora	11.60	16.46	1.42
Shareef Dancer	Northern Dancer	6.17	8.70	1.41
Machiavellian	Mr Prospector	17.87	25.00	1.40
Prince Sabo	Young Generation	7.98	11.15	1.40
Efisio	Formidable	11.11	15.31	1.38

Form Sires

DAMSIRE	DAMSIRE'S SIRE	OSR	RULE	IMP
Try My Best	Northern Dancer	8.38	18.37	2.19
Mr Prospector	Raise A Native	12.94	28.07	2.17
Rainbow Quest	Blushing Groom	14.40	29.41	2.04
Relkino	Relko	9.64	19.48	2.02
Lyphard	Northern Dancer	13.68	26.92	1.97
Ballad Rock	Bold Lad (IRE)	7.79	14.61	1.88
Mummy's Pet	Sing Sing	8.06	14.75	1.83
Rarity	Hethersett	13.71	24.00	1.75
Artaius	Round Table	9.86	17.07	1.73
The Minstrel	Northern Dancer	11.37	19.57	1.72
Seattle Slew	Bold Reasoning	12.57	20.69	1.65
Main Reef	Mill Reef	8.48	13.43	1.58
Welsh Saint	Sir Paddy	7.89	12.07	1.53
Arctic Tern	Sea-Bird II	14.04	21.43	1.53
Ela-Mana-Mou	Pitcairn	10.50	15.49	1.48
Dance In Time	Northern Dancer	10.86	15.91	1.46
Alzao	Lyphard	11.07	16.22	1.46
Kris	Sharpen Up	11.52	16.82	1.46
Red Sunset	Red God	8.80	12.50	1.42
Pharly	Lyphard	11.58	16.33	1.41
Nureyev	Northern Dancer	11.52	15.94	1.38
Diesis	Sharpen Up	10.70	14.55	1.36
Habitat	Sir Gaylord	11.31	15.13	1.34
Niniski	Nijinsky	9.13	12.12	1.33
Bay Express	Polyfoto	9.24	12.26	1.33
Red Alert	Red God	11.31	14.93	1.32
Auction Ring	Bold Bidder	8.54	11.23	1.31
Thatching	Thatch	9.96	13.04	1.31
Northern Dancer	Nearctic	15.30	20.00	1.31
Sharpen Up	Atan	10.51	13.71	1.30

Form Sires

SIRE	SIRE'S SIRE	WINS	RUNS	SR%
Nashwan	Blushing Groom	22	77	28.57
Mr Prospector	Raise A Native	8	29	27.59
El Gran Senor	Northern Dancer	19	69	27.54
Danzig	Northern Dancer	10	38	26.32
Machiavellian	Mr Prospector	15	59	25.42
Bering	Arctic Tern	8	34	23.53
Selkirk	Sharpen Up	14	62	22.58
Elmaamul	Diesis	16	71	22.54
Diesis	Sharpen Up	17	76	22.37
Groom Dancer	Blushing Groom	12	54	22.22
Nureyev	Northern Dancer	11	50	22.00
Generous	Caerleon	22	101	21.78
Sadler's Wells	Northern Dancer	22	113	19.47
Tragic Role	Nureyev	8	42	19.05
Gone West	Mr Prospector	8	43	18.60
Royal Academy	Nijinsky	30	165	18.18
Unfuwain	Northern Dancer	17	97	17.53
Ela-Mana-Mou	Pitcairn	8	46	17.39
Polar Falcon	Nureyev	14	81	17.28
Shaadi	Danzig	7	41	17.07
Doyoun	Mill Reef	9	54	16.67
Warning	Known Fact	22	133	16.54
Slip Anchor	Shirley Heights	14	85	16.47
Darshaan	Shirley Heights	12	73	16.44
Zilzal	Nureyev	8	49	16.33
Known Fact	In Reality	4	25	16.00
Sayf El Arab	Drone	4	25	16.00
Silver Hawk	Roberto	11	70	15.71
Woodman	Mr Prospector	17	109	15.60

Form Sires

DAMSIRE	DAMSIRE'S SIRE	WINS	RUNS	SR%
Exclusive Native	Raise A Native	8	33	24.24
Shirley Heights	Mill Reef	34	153	22.22
Nebbiolo	Yellow God	5	23	21.74
Darshaan	Shirley Heights	5	24	20.83
Topsider	Northern Dancer	4	20	20.00
Danzig	Northern Dancer	7	36	19.44
Secretariat	Bold Ruler	7	36	19.44
Irish River	Riverman	13	69	18.84
Sadler's Wells	Northern Dancer	14	75	18.67
Nureyev	Northern Dancer	13	70	18.57
Rousillon	Riverman	5	28	17.86
Mr Prospector	Raise A Native	11	64	17.19
Affirmed	Exclusive Native	6	35	17.14
Welsh Pageant	Tudor Melody	18	108	16.67
Riverman	Never Bend	13	80	16.25
Luthier	Klairon	4	26	15.38
Kris	Sharpen Up	22	144	15.28
Blushing Groom	Red God	15	101	14.85
Lomond	Northern Dancer	8	54	14.81
Chief Singer	Ballad Rock	5	34	14.71
Secreto	Northern Dancer	5	34	14.71
Green Dancer	Nijinsky	9	64	14.06
Habitat	Sir Gaylord	29	208	13.94
Persian Bold	Bold Lad (IRE)	16	115	13.91
Lyphard	Northern Dancer	12	87	13.79
Dancing Brave	Lyphard	3	22	13.64
Miswaki	Mr Prospector	3	22	13.64
Mill Reef	Never Bend	19	140	13.57
The Minstrel	Northern Dancer	12	95	12.63

Form Sires

SIRE	SIRE'S SIRE	OSR	RULE	IMP
Elmaamul	Diesis	11.72	22.54	1.92
Bering	Arctic Tern	12.96	23.53	1.82
El Gran Senor	Northern Dancer	15.40	27.54	1.79
Nashwan	Blushing Groom	16.31	28.57	1.75
Ballad Rock	Bold Lad (IRE)	6.98	11.63	1.67
Groom Dancer	Blushing Groom	13.84	22.22	1.61
Petorius	Mummy's Pet	8.46	13.04	1.54
Diesis	Sharpen Up	15.05	22.37	1.49
Fairy King	Northern Dancer	13.13	19.47	1.48
Tragic Role	Nureyev	12.89	19.05	1.48
Machiavellian	Mr Prospector	17.87	25.42	1.42
Sayf El Arab	Drone	11.37	16.00	1.41
Slip Anchor	Shirley Heights	12.14	16.47	1.36
Weldnaas	Diesis	6.19	8.33	1.35
Rock City	Ballad Rock	9.77	13.01	1.33
Royal Academy	Nijinsky	13.71	18.18	1.33
Unfuwain	Northern Dancer	13.58	17.53	1.29
Last Tycoon	Try My Best	11.22	14.29	1.27
Tirol	Thatching	8.81	11.11	1.26
Known Fact	In Reality	12.80	16.00	1.25
Darshaan	Shirley Heights	13.24	16.44	1.24
Mr Prospector	Raise A Native	22.30	27.59	1.24
Danzig	Northern Dancer	21.36	26.32	1.23
Warning	Known Fact	13.47	16.54	1.23
Selkirk	Sharpen Up	18.41	22.58	1.23
Shaadi	Danzig	14.01	17.07	1.22
Prince Sabo	Young Generation	7.98	9.71	1.22
Alzao	Lyphard	12.23	14.86	1.21
Fayruz	Song	8.25	10.00	1.21
Thatching	Thatch	9.02	10.77	1.19

Form Sires

DAMSIRE	DAMSIRE'S SIRE	OSR	RULE	IMP
Nebbiolo	Yellow God	11.92	21.74	1.82
Secretariat	Bold Ruler	10.96	19.44	1.77
Shirley Heights	Mill Reef	12.97	22.22	1.71
Welsh Pageant	Tudor Melody	10.19	16.67	1.64
Nureyev	Northern Dancer	11.52	18.57	1.61
Lomond	Northern Dancer	9.80	14.81	1.51
Mummy's Pet	Sing Sing	8.06	11.51	1.43
Irish River	Riverman	13.27	18.84	1.42
Darshaan	Shirley Heights	14.73	20.83	1.41
Ballad Rock	Bold Lad (IRE)	7.79	10.91	1.40
Luthier	Klairon	11.11	15.38	1.38
Mr Prospector	Raise A Native	12.94	17.19	1.33
Kris	Sharpen Up	11.52	15.28	1.33
Danzig	Northern Dancer	14.79	19.44	1.31
Sallust	Pall Mall	8.26	10.66	1.29
Persian Bold	Bold Lad (IRE)	10.93	13.91	1.27
Habitat	Sir Gaylord	11.31	13.94	1.23
Pas De Seul	Mill Reef	11.51	14.06	1.22
Green Dancer	Nijinsky	12.00	14.63	1.22
Riverman	Never Bend	13.44	16.25	1.21
Blushing Groom	Red God	12.30	14.85	1.21
Chief Singer	Ballad Rock	12.27	14.71	1.20
Topsider	Northern Dancer	17.21	20.00	1.16
Affirmed	Exclusive Native	14.81	17.14	1.16
Relkino	Relko	9.64	11.11	1.15
Miswaki	Mr Prospector	11.90	13.64	1.15
Exclusive Native	Raise A Native	21.30	24.24	1.14
Sadler's Wells	Northern Dancer	16.46	18.67	1.13
Rousillon	Riverman	15.83	17.86	1.13
The Minstrel	Northern Dancer	11.37	12.63	1.11

Form Sires

SIRE	SIRE'S SIRE	WINS	RUNS	SR%
Nureyev	Northern Dancer	10	54	18.52
Danzig	Northern Dancer	17	92	18.48
Safawan	Young Generation	15	82	18.29
Most Welcome	Be My Guest	19	109	17.43
Royal Academy	Nijinsky	20	119	16.81
Bluebird	Storm Bird	31	187	16.58
Storm Cat	Storm Bird	12	73	16.44
Cadeaux Genereux	Young Generation	44	271	16.24
Dayjur	Danzig	13	81	16.05
Last Tycoon	Try My Best	21	132	15.91
Nordico	Northern Dancer	23	155	14.84
Distant Relative	Habitat	34	234	14.53
Green Desert	Danzig	38	263	14.45
Dashing Blade	Elegant Air	15	104	14.42
Damister	Mr Prospector	11	77	14.29
Distinctly North	Minshaanshu Amad	19	139	13.67
Efisio	Formidable	75	562	13.35
Pharly	Lyphard	10	75	13.33
Night Shift	Northern Dancer	48	372	12.90
Tirol	Thatching	10	78	12.82
Polish Patriot	Danzig	14	111	12.61
Dowsing	Riverman	46	373	12.33
Ballacashtal	Vice Regent	14	115	12.17
Komaite	Nureyev	33	281	11.74
Reprimand	Mummy's Pet	25	215	11.63
Warning	Known Fact	25	216	11.57
Never So Bold	Bold Lad (IRE)	34	297	11.45
Thatching	Thatch	37	328	11.28
Fairy King	Northern Dancer	38	341	11.14
Sharpo	Sharpen Up	43	396	10.86

Form Sires

DAMSIRE	DAMSIRE'S SIRE	WINS	RUNS	SR%
Caro	Fortino II	11	53	20.75
Reform	Pall Mall	19	94	20.21
Ile De Bourbon	Nijinsky	16	85	18.82
Mount Hagen	Bold Bidder	11	63	17.46
Indian King	Raja Baba	22	128	17.19
Irish River	Riverman	11	67	16.42
Riverman	Never Bend	18	117	15.38
Ela-Mana-Mou	Pitcairn	11	77	14.29
Persian Bold	Bold Lad (IRE)	14	101	13.86
High Top	Derring-Do	19	140	13.57
Red Alert	Red God	22	164	13.41
Northfields	Northern Dancer	25	203	12.32
Lochnager	Dumbarnie	28	228	12.28
Nebbiolo	Yellow God	16	134	11.94
Blakeney	Hethersett	12	103	11.65
Artaius	Round Table	15	130	11.54
Sharpen Up	Atan	23	212	10.85
Godswalk	Dancer's Image	17	159	10.69
Known Fact	In Reality	19	181	10.50
Ahonoora	Lorenzaccio	12	115	10.43
Music Boy	Jukebox	29	285	10.18
Lord Gayle	Sir Gaylord	17	172	9.88
Star Appeal	Appiani II	12	125	9.60
Song	Sing Sing	37	390	9.49
Bay Express	Polyfoto	20	212	9.43
Thatching	Thatch	15	159	9.43
Try My Best	Northern Dancer	19	205	9.27
Dominion	Derring-Do	25	277	9.03
Be My Guest	Northern Dancer	25	283	8.83
Welsh Saint	Sir Paddy	14	174	8.05

Form Sires

SIRE	SIRE'S SIRE	OSR	RULE	IMP
Tirol	Thatching	7.05	12.82	1.82
Nordico	Northern Dancer	8.88	14.84	1.67
Safawan	Young Generation	10.99	18.29	1.66
Distinctly North	Minshaanshu Amad	8.57	13.67	1.60
Ballacashtal	Vice Regent	8.24	12.17	1.48
Last Tycoon	Try My Best	10.78	15.91	1.48
Hadeer	General Assembly	7.11	10.18	1.43
Never So Bold	Bold Lad (IRE)	8.03	11.45	1.43
Bluebird	Storm Bird	12.02	16.58	1.38
Damister	Mr Prospector	10.43	14.29	1.37
Royal Academy	Nijinsky	12.35	16.81	1.36
Thatching	Thatch	8.38	11.28	1.35
Ballad Rock	Bold Lad (IRE)	6.21	8.36	1.35
Efisio	Formidable	10.42	13.35	1.28
Reprimand	Mummy's Pet	9.09	11.63	1.28
Most Welcome	Be My Guest	13.74	17.43	1.27
Pharly	Lyphard	10.69	13.33	1.25
Distant Relative	Habitat	11.85	14.53	1.23
Dayjur	Danzig	13.16	16.05	1.22
Aragon	Mummy's Pet	7.81	9.42	1.21
Primo Dominie	Dominion	8.68	10.43	1.20
Statoblest	Ahonoora	8.67	10.40	1.20
Formidable	Forli	7.84	9.39	1.20
Cadeaux G'nereux	Young Generation	13.68	16.24	1.19
Night Shift	Northern Dancer	10.89	12.90	1.18
Komaite	Nureyev	10.00	11.74	1.17
Green Desert	Danzig	12.44	14.45	1.16
Prince Sabo	Young Generation	6.55	7.43	1.13
Interrex	Vice Regent	9.40	10.56	1.12

Form Sires

DAMSIRE	DAMSIRE'S SIRE	OSR	RULE	IMP
Reform	Pall Mall	12.09	20.21	1.67
Indian King	Raja Baba	10.60	17.19	1.62
Caro	Fortino II	12.84	20.75	1.62
Ile De Bourbon	Nijinsky	12.01	18.82	1.57
Ela-Mana-Mou	Pitcairn	10.14	14.29	1.41
Blakeney	Hethersett	8.90	11.65	1.31
Irish River	Riverman	12.74	16.42	1.29
Persian Bold	Bold Lad (IRE)	10.94	13.86	1.27
Lord Gayle	Sir Gaylord	7.98	9.88	1.24
Try My Best	Northern Dancer	7.60	9.27	1.22
Bay Express	Polyfoto	8.04	9.43	1.17
Riverman	Never Bend	13.12	15.38	1.17
Lochnager	Dumbarnie	10.54	12.28	1.17
Artaius	Round Table	9.91	11.54	1.16
Northfields	Northern Dancer	10.64	12.32	1.16
Red Alert	Red God	11.64	13.41	1.15
Song	Sing Sing	8.35	9.49	1.14
Mummy's Pet	Sing Sing	6.19	7.04	1.14
Godswalk	Dancer's Image	9.46	10.69	1.13
High Top	Derring-Do	12.12	13.57	1.12
Sharpen Up	Atan	10.14	10.85	1.07
Welsh Saint	Sir Paddy	7.62	8.05	1.06
Mount Hagen	Bold Bidder	16.67	17.46	1.05
Known Fact	In Reality	10.25	10.50	1.02
Music Boy	Jukebox	9.47	9.43	1.00

Form Sires

SIRE	SIRE'S SIRE	WINS	RUNS	SR%
Nureyev	Northern Dancer	52	221	23.53
Storm Cat	Storm Bird	23	112	20.54
Mr Prospector	Raise A Native	26	131	19.85
Red Ransom	Roberto	11	56	19.64
Sadler's Wells	Northern Dancer	35	198	17.68
Zilzal	Nureyev	33	188	17.55
Selkirk	Sharpen Up	14	81	17.28
Danzig	Northern Dancer	30	176	17.05
Soviet Star	Nureyev	61	361	16.90
Doyoun	Mill Reef	13	78	16.67
Lear Fan	Roberto	25	151	16.56
Shaadi	Danzig	42	258	16.28
Danehill	Danzig	89	550	16.18
Gone West	Mr Prospector	25	163	15.34
Rainbow Quest	Blushing Groom	34	226	15.04
El Gran Senor	Northern Dancer	32	217	14.75
Polish Precedent	Danzig	30	204	14.71
Warning	Known Fact	76	522	14.56
Polar Falcon	Nureyev	23	158	14.56
Caerleon	Nijinsky	30	213	14.08
Shalford	Thatching	13	93	13.98
Alzao	Lyphard	58	415	13.98
Dixieland Band	Northern Dancer	14	102	13.73
Bluebird	Storm Bird	53	391	13.55
Sayf El Arab	Drone	21	156	13.46
Royal Academy	Nijinsky	53	394	13.45
Woodman	Mr Prospector	28	209	13.40
Most Welcome	Be My Guest	51	381	13.39
Nashwan	Blushing Groom	23	172	13.37
Cadeaux Genereux	Young Generation	71	537	13.22

Form Sires

DAMSIRE	DAMSIRE'S SIRE	WINS	RUNS	SR%
Exclusive Native	Raise A Native	11	51	21.57
Topsider	Northern Dancer	12	59	20.34
Bellypha	Lyphard	13	65	20.00
Northern Dancer	Nearctic	29	163	17.79
Mount Hagen	Bold Bidder	15	89	16.85
Troy	Petingo	28	167	16.77
Sadler's Wells	Northern Dancer	11	68	16.18
Riverman	Never Bend	27	175	15.43
Affirmed	Exclusive Native	15	99	15.15
Seattle Slew	Bold Reasoning	20	138	14.49
General Assembly	Secretariat	23	165	13.94
Vaguely Noble	Vienna	38	273	13.92
Hot Spark	Habitat	12	87	13.79
High Line	High Hat	38	278	13.67
Shareef Dancer	Northern Dancer	21	156	13.46
Mill Reef	Never Bend	40	298	13.42
Rarity	Hethersett	11	84	13.10
Nijinsky	Northern Dancer	26	200	13.00
Secretariat	Bold Ruler	23	177	12.99
Top Ville	High Top	10	78	12.82
Persian Bold	Bold Lad (IRE)	29	227	12.78
Roberto	Hail To Reason	13	104	12.50
Irish River	Riverman	21	169	12.43
Hotfoot	Firestreak	24	195	12.31
Luthier	Klairon	13	108	12.04
Arctic Tern	Sea-Bird II	20	168	11.90
Secreto	Northern Dancer	10	84	11.90
Pas De Seul	Mill Reef	31	262	11.83
Habat	Habitat	15	127	11.81
Be My Guest	Northern Dancer	48	411	11.68

Form Sires

SIRE - IMPROVEMENT TABLE - MILE (3 y-o+)

SIRE	SIRE'S SIRE	OSR	RULE	IMP
Imp Society	Barrera	9.17	12.28	1.34
Be My Chief	Chief's Crown	9.40	12.35	1.31
Anshan	Persian Bold	8.03	10.43	1.30
Rambo Dancer	Northern Dancer	8.58	11.04	1.29
Rock City	Ballad Rock	10.14	12.93	1.27
Fayruz	Song	7.26	9.19	1.27
Pennine Walk	Persian Bold	9.73	12.24	1.26
Mazilier	Lyphard	9.27	11.57	1.25
Lear Fan	Roberto	13.27	16.56	1.25
Warning	Known Fact	11.83	14.56	1.23
Shalford	Thatching	11.36	13.98	1.23
Nomination	Dominion	6.70	8.15	1.22
Sayf El Arab	Drone	11.21	13.46	1.20
Storm Cat	Storm Bird	17.27	20.54	1.19
Shaadi	Danzig	13.75	16.28	1.18
Red Ransom	Roberto	16.67	19.64	1.18
Alzao	Lyphard	11.97	13.98	1.17
Imperial Frontier	Lyphard	7.31	8.50	1.16
Danehill	Danzig	14.04	16.18	1.15
Nordico	Northern Dancer	8.88	10.19	1.15
Soviet Star	Nureyev	14.94	16.90	1.13
Bluebird	Storm Bird	12.02	13.55	1.13
Gone West	Mr Prospector	13.78	15.34	1.11
Doyoun	Mill Reef	14.98	16.67	1.11
El Gran Senor	Northern Dancer	13.27	14.75	1.11
Forzando	Formidable	8.88	9.77	1.10
Irish River	Riverman	9.41	10.31	1.10
Zilzal	Nureyev	16.05	17.55	1.09
Royal Academy	Nijinsky	12.35	13.45	1.09
Indian Ridge	Ahonoora	10.61	11.56	1.09

Form Sires

DAMSIRE	DAMSIRE'S SIRE	OSR	RULE	IMP
Bellypha	Lyphard	13.98	20.00	1.43
Runnett	Mummy's Pet	7.51	10.19	1.36
Habat	Habitat	9.02	11.81	1.31
Troy	Petingo	13.07	16.77	1.28
Nonoalco	Nearctic	9.13	11.68	1.28
Lomond	Northern Dancer	8.37	10.43	1.25
Affirmed	Exclusive Native	12.50	15.15	1.21
Vaguely Noble	Vienna	11.60	13.92	1.20
Riverman	Never Bend	13.12	15.43	1.18
Secretariat	Bold Ruler	11.08	12.99	1.17
Persian Bold	Bold Lad (IRE)	10.94	12.78	1.17
Topsider	Northern Dancer	17.47	20.34	1.16
Northern Dancer	Nearctic	15.37	17.79	1.16
Known Fact	In Reality	10.25	11.50	1.12
Red Sunset	Red God	8.46	9.45	1.12
Caerleon	Nijinsky	8.88	9.87	1.11
Exclusive Native	Raise A Native	19.67	21.57	1.10
Music Boy	Jukebox	9.95	10.81	1.09
High Line	High Hat	12.69	13.67	1.08
Nureyev	Northern Dancer	9.22	9.84	1.07
Pas De Seul	Mill Reef	11.09	11.83	1.07
Kings Lake	Nijinsky	9.70	10.30	1.06
General Assembly	Secretariat	13.17	13.94	1.06
Formidable	Forli	10.07	10.63	1.06
Kris	Sharpen Up	10.34	10.86	1.05
Sadler's Wells	Northern Dancer	15.61	16.18	1.04
Top Ville	High Top	12.38	12.82	1.04
Luthier	Klairon	11.63	12.04	1.04
Bay Express	Polyfoto	8.04	8.29	1.03
Seattle Slew	Bold Reasoning	14.17	14.49	1.02

Form Sires

SIRE	SIRES-SIRE	WINS	RUNS	SR%
Known Fact	In Reality	15	58	25.86
Danzig	Northern Dancer	27	110	24.55
Clantime	Music Boy	18	75	24.00
Nureyev	Northern Dancer	24	101	23.76
Alleged	Hoist The Flag	48	228	21.05
Priolo	Sovereign Dancer	19	97	19.59
Sadler's Wells	Northern Dancer	172	904	19.03
Generous	Caerleon	33	177	18.64
Polish Patriot	Danzig	12	65	18.46
Manila	Lyphard	11	68	16.18
Rainbow Quest	Blushing Groom	92	571	16.11
Caerleon	Nijinsky	64	400	16.00
Rousillon	Riverman	39	245	15.92
Doyoun	Mill Reef	14	88	15.91
In The Wings	Sadler's Wells	37	234	15.81
Zilzal	Nureyev	14	91	15.38
Sharrood	Caro	39	258	15.12
Broken Hearted	Dara Monarch	23	153	15.03
Kalaglow	Kalamoun	36	240	15.00
Green Dancer	Nijinsky	15	101	14.85
Diesis	Sharpen Up	30	205	14.63
Shaadi	Danzig	15	103	14.56
Most Welcome	Be My Guest	44	304	14.47
Kahyasi	Ile De Bourbon	22	154	14.29
Old Vic	Sadler's Wells	31	218	14.22
Polish Precedent	Danzig	35	252	13.89
Riverman	Never Bend	23	166	13.86
Dominion	Derring-Do	35	254	13.78
Silver Hawk	Roberto	35	255	13.73
Last Tycoon	Try My Best	44	322	13.66

Form Sires

DAMSIRE	DAMSIRE'S SIRE	WINS	RUNS	SR%
Halo	Hail To Reason	10	31	32.26
Shareef Dancer	Northern Dancer	20	81	24.69
Dance In Time	Northern Dancer	11	55	20.00
Shirley Heights	Mill Reef	36	186	19.35
Kalaglow	Kalamoun	10	52	19.23
Mill Reef	Never Bend	43	226	19.03
Top Ville	High Top	13	69	18.84
Northern Dancer	Nearctic	15	83	18.07
Sadler's Wells	Northern Dancer	10	56	17.86
Nijinsky	Northern Dancer	27	156	17.31
Busted	Crepello	30 ·	182	16.48
Grundy	Great Nephew	21	129	16.28
Mr Prospector	Raise A Native	12	81	14.81
Star Appeal	Appiani II	22	151	14.57
Roberto	Hail To Reason	12	86	13.95
Blushing Groom	Red God	15	113	13.27
High Top	Derring-Do	39	295	13.22
Great Nephew	Honeyway	16	122	13.11
Green Dancer	Nijinsky	14	107	13.08
Be My Guest	Northern Dancer	20	156	12.82
The Minstrel	Northern Dancer	12	95	12.63
Caro	Fortino II	15	121	12.40
Dominion	Derring-Do	12	100	12.00
High Line	High Hat	13	109	11.93
Lyphard	Northern Dancer	14	120	11.67
Riverman	Never Bend	13	112	11.61
Blakeney	Hethersett	25	218	11.47
Sallust	Pall Mall	11	97	11.34
Habitat	Sir Gaylord	27	239	11.30

Form Sires

SIRE	SIRE'S SIRE	OSR	RULE	IMP
Clantime	Music Boy	10.28	24.00	2.33
Known Fact	In Reality	12.17	25.86	2.12
Polish Patriot	Danzig	12.71	18.46	1.45
Superlative	Nebbiolo	9.46	13.48	1.43
Priolo	Sovereign Dancer	14.05	19.59	1.39
Riverman	Never Bend	10.21	13.86	1.36
Weldnaas	Diesis	6.15	8.33	1.35
Petorius	Mummy's Pet	7.95	10.59	1.33
Keen	Sharpen Up	8.12	10.71	1.32
Dominion	Derring-Do	10.52	13.78	1.31
Danzig	Northern Dancer	19.02	24.55	1.29
Kahyasi	Ile De Bourbon	11.14	14.29	1.28
Last Tycoon	Try My Best	10.78	13.66	1.27
Rousillon	Riverman	12.85	15.92	1.24
Sharrood	Caro	12.33	15.12	1.23
Broken Hearted	Dara Monarch	12.27	15.03	1.23
Indian Ridge	Ahonoora	10.61	12.78	1.20
Tragic Role	Nureyev	11.30	13.54	1.20
Red Sunset	Red God	9.87	11.64	1.18
Shareef Dancer	Northern Dancer	6.21	7.32	1.18
Bairn	Northern Baby	9.73	11.45	1.18
Don't Forget Me	Ahonoora	7.11	8.36	1.18
Never So Bold	Bold Lad (IRE)	8.03	9.42	1.17
Kris	Sharpen Up	11.38	13.30	1.17
Be My Guest	Northern Dancer	11.49	13.26	1.15
Damister	Mr Prospector	10.43	11.80	1.13
Mazilier	Lyphard	9.27	10.48	1.13
Alleged	Hoist The Flag	18.70	21.05	1.13
Old Vic	Sadler's Wells	12.71	14.22	1.12
Kalaglow	Kalamoun	13.47	15.00	1.11

Form Sires

DAMSIRE	DAMSIRE'S SIRE	OSR	RULE	IMP
Halo	Hail To Reason	13.61	32.26	2.37
Dance In Time	Northern Dancer	10.07	20.00	1.99
Mummy's Pet	Sing Sing	6.19	12.00	1.94
Shareef Dancer	Northern Dancer	14.02	24.69	1.76
Grundy	Great Nephew	9.60	16.28	1.70
Shirley Heights	Mill Reef	12.00	19.35	1.61
Top Ville	High Top	12.38	18.84	1.52
Star Appeal	Appiani II	9.71	14.57	1.50
Busted	Crepello	11.02	16.48	1.50
Sallust	Pall Mall	7.91	11.34	1.43
Mr Prospector	Raise A Native	10.56	14.81	1.40
Kalaglow	Kalamoun	13.96	19.23	1.38
Great Nephew	Honeyway	10.00	13.11	1.31
Blakeney	Hethersett	8.90	11.47	1.29
Bustino	Busted	8.96	11.23	1.25
Dominion	Derring-Do	9.92	12.32	1.24
The Minstrel	Northern Dancer	10.34	12.63	1.22
Nijinsky	Northern Dancer	14.42	17.31	1.20
Northern Dancer	Nearctic	15.37	18.07	1.18
Mill Reef	Never Bend	16.57	19.03	1.15
Sadler's Wells	Northern Dancer	15.61	17.86	1.14
Be My Guest	Northern Dancer	11.43	12.82	1.12
Formidable	Forli	10.07	11.11	1.10
Habitat	Sir Gaylord	10.34	11.30	1.09
Sir Ivor	Sir Gaylord	9.24	10.08	1.09
High Top	Derring-Do	12.12	13.22	1.09
Sharpen Up	Atan	10.14	11.01	1.09
Green Dancer	Nijinsky	12.07	13.08	1.08
Blushing Groom	Red God	12.27	13.27	1.08
Lyphard	Northern Dancer	11.61	11.67	1.00

Form Sires

SIRE	SIRE'S SIRE	WINS	RUNS	SR%
Generous	Caerleon	15	59	25.42
Ela-Mana-Mou	Pitcairn	41	197	20.81
Green Dancer	Nijinsky	11	54	20.37
Caerleon	Nijinsky	34	170	20.00
Alleged	Hoist The Flag	15	82	18.29
Woodman	Mr Prospector	10	59	16.95
Sadler's Wells	Northern Dancer	41	244	16.80
High Estate	Shirley Heights	9	55	16.36
Unfuwain	Northern Dancer	18	111	16.22
Mtoto	Busted	23	145	15.86
Lear Fan	Roberto	12	77	15.58
Persian Bold	Bold Lad (IRE)	11	72	15.28
Old Vic	Sadler's Wells	17	114	14.91
Darshaan	Shirley Heights	18	121	14.88
Salse	Topsider	25	172	14.53
Shirley Heights	Mill Reef	31	217	14.29
Kalaglow	Kalamoun	9	64	14.06
In The Wings	Sadler's Wells	12	89	13.48
Pharly	Lyphard	21	158	13.29
Petoski	Niniski	12	92	13.04
Be My Guest	Northern Dancer	10	77	12.99
Rousillon	Riverman	11	85	12.94
Slip Anchor	Shirley Heights	37	290	12.76
Bairn	Northern Baby	9	72	12.50
Rainbow Quest	Blushing Groom	22	181	12.15
Sharrood	Caro	12	100	12.00
Don't Forget Me	Ahonoora	10	84	11.90
Robellino	Roberto	10	86	11.63
Alzao	Lyphard	13	127	10.24
Kahyasi	Ile De Bourbon	13	134	9.70

Form Sires

DAMSIRE	DAMSIRE'S SIRE	WINS	RUNS	SR%
Hotfoot	Firestreak	19	66	28.79
Mill Reef	Never Bend	19	96	19.79
Welsh Pageant	Tudor Melody	24	125	19.20
Blushing Groom	Red God	24	141	17.02
Ile De Bourbon	Nijinsky	12	75	16.00
The Minstrel	Northern Dancer	9	57	15.79
Artaius	Round Table	10	70	14.29
High Line	High Hat	10	71	14.08
Habitat	Sir Gaylord	19	144	13.19
Be My Guest	Northern Dancer	18	144	12.50
Shirley Heights	Mill Reef	14	116	12.07
Green Dancer	Nijinsky	14	120	11.67
Blakeney	Hethersett	20	184	10.87
Sir Ivor	Sir Gaylord	8	75	10.67
Grundy	Great Nephew	10	95	10.53
Busted	Crepello	12	116	10.34
Bustino	Busted	11	110	10.00
Troy	Petingo	9	92	9.78
Vaguely Noble	Vienna	12	126	9.52
High Top	Derring-Do	13	154	8.44

Form Sires

SIRE	SIRE'S SIRE	OSR	RULE	IMP
Don't Forget Me	Ahonoora	7.11	11.90	1.67
High Estate	Shirley Heights	9.88	16.36	1.66
Ela-Mana-Mou	Pitcairn	15.75	20.81	1.32
Woodman	Mr Prospector	12.89	16.95	1.31
Green Dancer	Nijinsky	15.52	20.37	1.31
Generous	Caerleon	19.45	25.42	1.31
Bairn	Northern Baby	9.73	12.50	1.28
Persian Bold	Bold Lad (IRE)	12.20	15.28	1.25
Petoski	Niniski	10.43	13.04	1.25
Unfuwain	Northern Dancer	12.98	16.22	1.25
Caerleon	Nijinsky	16.02	20.00	1.25
Pharly	Lyphard	10.69	13.29	1.24
Mtoto	Busted	12.80	15.86	1.24
Salse	Topsider	11.85	14.53	1.23
Darshaan	Shirley Heights	12.67	14.88	1.17
Lear Fan	Roberto	13.27	15.58	1.17
Old Vic	Sadler's Wells	12.71	14.91	1.17
Be My Guest	Northern Dancer	11.49	12.99	1.13
Robellino	Roberto	10.45	11.63	1.11
Slip Anchor	Shirley Heights	11.70	12.76	1.09
Shirley Heights	Mill Reef	13.25	14.29	1.08
Kalaglow	Kalamoun	13.47	14.06	1.04
Rousillon	Riverman	12.85	12.94	1.01

Form Sires

DAMSIRE	DAMSIRE'S SIRE	OSR	RULE	IMP
Hotfoot	Firestreak	12.61	28.79	2.28
Welsh Pageant	Tudor Melody	9.01	19.20	2.13
The Minstrel	Northern Dancer	10.34	15.79	1.53
Artaius	Round Table	9.91	14.29	1.44
Blushing Groom	Red God	12.27	17.02	1.39
Ile De Bourbon	Nijinsky	12.01	16.00	1.33
Habitat	Sir Gaylord	10.34	13.19	1.28
Blakeney	Hethersett	8.90	10.87	1.22
Mill Reef	Never Bend	16.57	19.79	1.19
Sir Ivor	Sir Gaylord	9.24	10.67	1.15
Bustino	Busted	8.96	10.00	1.12
High Line	High Hat	12.69	14.08	1.11
Grundy	Great Nephew	9.60	10.53	1.10
Be My Guest	Northern Dancer	11.43	12.50	1.09
Shirley Heights	Mill Reef	12.00	12.07	1.01

Form Sires

Chapter 8

Performance Tables: Weight Carrying Ability

SIRE - CONSISTENCY TABLE - WEIGHT

SIRE	SIRE'S SIRE	WINS	RUNS	SR%
Generous	Caerleon	10	23	43.48
Storm Cat	Storm Bird	9	34	26.47
Tragic Role	Nureyev	8	32	25.00
Try My Best	Northern Dancer	19	81	23.46
Polish Patriot	Danzig	10	43	23.26
El Gran Senor	Northern Dancer	11	49	22.45
Nureyev	Northern Dancer	9	44	20.45
Rock City	Ballad Rock	11	54	20.37
Danzig	Northern Dancer	11	57	19.30
Kefaah	Blushing Groom	9	47	19.15
Clantime	Music Boy	28	149	18.79
Sharrood	Caro	16	86	18.60
Pharly	Lyphard	21	113	18.58
Sayf El Arab	Drone	14	76	18.42
Sadler's Wells	Northern Dancer	18	98	18.37
High Estate	Shirley Heights	8	44	18.18
Last Tycoon	Try My Best	19	117	16.24
Shirley Heights	Mill Reef	21	130	16.15
Cadeaux Genereux	Young Generation	25	158	15.82
Roi Danzig	Danzig	12	76	15.79
Superlative	Nebbiolo	13	84	15.48
Distant Relative	Habitat	11	72	15.28
Rousillon	Riverman	26	172	15.12
Bering	Arctic Tern	13	87	14.94
Caerleon	Nijinsky	17	115	14.78
Dominion	Derring-Do	23	156	14.74
Komaite	Nureyev	13	90	14.44
Alzao	Lyphard	24	169	14.20
Kalaglow	Kalamoun	13	92	14.13
Shaadi	Danzig	11	78	14.10

Form Sires

DAMSIRE - CONSISTENCY TABLE - WEIGHT

DAMSIRE	DAMSIRES-SIRE	WINS	RUNS	SR%
Irish River	Riverman	9	44	20.45
Lyphard	Northern Dancer	13	66	19.70
General Assembly	Secretariat	9	47	19.15
Red Alert	Red God	16	84	19.05
Mill Reef	Never Bend	18	96	18.75
Dance In Time	Northern Dancer	11	61	18.03
Seattle Slew	Bold Reasoning	9	53	16.98
Caro	Fortino II	10	59	16.95
Shirley Heights	Mill Reef	14	85	16.47
Top Ville	High Top	7	45	15.56
Sharpen Up	Atan	26	168	15.48
High Line	High Hat	15	99	15.15
Northfields	Northern Dancer	26	176	14.77
High Top	Derring-Do	26	177	14.69
Vaguely Noble	Vienna	16	110	14.55
Dominion	Derring-Do	16	111	14.41
Busted	Crepello	14	108	12.96
Try My Best	Northern Dancer	8	63	12.70
Be My Guest	Northern Dancer	24	189	12.70
Music Boy	Jukebox	11	90	12.22
Lord Gayle	Sir Gaylord	10	85	11.76
Sir Ivor	Sir Gaylord	10	86	11.63
Ile De Bourbon	Nijinsky	8	69	11.59
Troy	Petingo	9	78	11.54
Nijinsky	Northern Dancer	16	140	11.43
Great Nephew	Honeyway	8	71	11.27
Bay Express	Polyfoto	9	82	10.98
Nonoalco	Nearctic	8	74	10.81
Star Appeal	Appiani II	12	113	10.62
Bustino	Busted	12	115	10.43

Form Sires

SIRE	SIRE'S SIRE	OSR	RULE	IMP
Try My Best	Northern Dancer	9.51	23.46	2.47
Generous	Caerleon	19.90	43.48	2.18
Rock City	Ballad Rock	9.77	20.37	2.08
Clantime	Music Boy	9.30	18.79	2.02
Shareef Dancer	Northern Dancer	6.17	12.38	2.01
Tragic Role	Nureyev	12.89	25.00	1.94
Polish Patriot	Danzig	12.19	23.26	1.91
High Estate	Shirley Heights	9.85	18.18	1.85
Kefaah	Blushing Groom	10.86	19.15	1.76
Pharly	Lyphard	10.57	18.58	1.76
Superlative	Nebbiolo	9.16	15.48	1.69
Ballacashtal	Vice Regent	8.09	13.41	1.66
Sayf El Arab	Drone	11.37	18.42	1.62
Tina's Pet	Mummy's Pet	7.42	11.61	1.56
Sharrood	Caro	12.06	18.60	1.54
Hadeer	General Assembly	6.89	10.58	1.54
Rambo Dancer	Northern Dancer	8.29	12.70	1.53
Roi Danzig	Danzig	10.62	15.79	1.49
Storm Cat	Storm Bird	17.96	26.47	1.47
Dominion	Derring-Do	10.07	14.74	1.46
El Gran Senor	Northern Dancer	15.40	22.45	1.46
Last Tycoon	Try My Best	11.22	16.24	1.45
Doulab	Topsider	9.40	13.58	1.44
Reprimand	Mummy's Pet	9.14	12.93	1.41
Petorius	Mummy's Pet	8.46	11.76	1.39
Don't Forget Me	Ahonoora	7.41	10.00	1.35
Forzando	Formidable	9.21	12.12	1.32
Distant Relative	Habitat	11.68	15.28	1.31
Cyrano De Bergerac	Bold Lad (IRE)	7.54	9.82	1.30
Bairn	Northern Baby	9.08	11.71	1.29

Form Sires

DAMSIRE - IMPROVEMENT TABLE - WEIGHT

DAMSIRE	DAMSIRE'S SIRE	OSR	RULE	IMP
Red Alert	Red God	11.31	19.05	1.68
Dance In Time	Northern Dancer	10.86	18.03	1.66
General Assembly	Secretariat	12.17	19.15	1.57
Irish River	Riverman	13.27	20.45	1.54
Lord Gayle	Sir Gaylord	7.68	11.76	1.53
Try My Best	Northern Dancer	8.38	12.70	1.52
Sharpen Up	Atan	10.51	15.48	1.47
Lyphard	Northern Dancer	13.68	19.70	1.44
Dominion	Derring-Do	10.09	14.41	1.43
Northfields	Northern Dancer	10.93	14.77	1.35
Seattle Slew	Bold Reasoning	12.57	16.98	1.35
Caro	Fortino II	12.62	16.95	1.34
Top Ville	High Top	11.69	15.56	1.33
Sir Ivor	Sir Gaylord	8.89	11.63	1.31
Vaguely Noble	Vienna	11.17	14.55	1.30
Great Nephew	Honeyway	8.74	11.27	1.29
Shirley Heights	Mill Reef	12.97	16.47	1.27
High Line	High Hat	12.07	15.15	1.26
Music Boy	Jukebox	9.82	12.22	1.24
Blakeney	Hethersett	8.13	9.93	1.22
High Top	Derring-Do	12.15	14.69	1.21
Busted	Crepello	10.74	12.96	1.21
Nonoalco	Nearctic	8.98	10.81	1.20
Bay Express	Polyfoto	9.24	10.98	1.19
Bustino	Busted	9.06	10.43	1.15
Mill Reef	Never Bend	16.29	18.75	1.15
Be My Guest	Northern Dancer	11.16	12.70	1.14
Star Appeal	Appiani II	9.44	10.62	1.12
Godswalk	Dancer's Image	8.45	8.79	1.04
Troy	Petingo	11.56	11.54	1.00

Form Sires

Chapter 9

Performance Tables: All-Weather Sires

SIRE - CONSISTENCY TABLE - AWT

SIRE	SIRE'S SIRE	WINS	RUNS	SR%
Nureyev	Northern Dancer	14	40	35.00
Storm Cat	Storm Bird	12	47	25.53
Lear Fan	Roberto	12	52	23.08
Danzig	Northern Dancer	107	501	21.36
Most Welcome	Be My Guest	31	146	21.23
Caerleon	Nijinsky	20	98	20.41
Warning	Known Fact	24	119	20.17
Polish Patriot	Danzig	16	80	20.00
Woodman	Mr Prospector	10	50	20.00
Lugana Beach	Tumble Wind	17	90	18.89
Rainbow Quest	Blushing Groom	30	159	18.87
Royal Academy	Nijinsky	13	79	16.46
Green Desert	Danzig	28	172	16.28
Keen	Sharpen Up	16	99	16.16
Kalaglow	Kalamoun	15	95	15.79
Alzao	Lyphard	28	181	15.47
Dowsing	Riverman	34	220	15.45
Petorius	Mummy's Pet	26	171	15.20
Unfuwain	Northern Dancer	10	67	14.93
Primo Dominie	Dominion	48	330	14.55
Komaite	Nureyev	39	271	14.39
Sharrood	Caro	16	113	14.16
Rock City	Ballad Rock	20	142	14.08
Distinctly North	Minshaanshu Amad	16	114	14.04
Damister	Mr Prospector	14	101	13.86
Shirley Heights	Mill Reef	10	73	13.70
Ballad Rock	Bold Lad (IRE)	13	95	13.68
Petoski	Niniski	15	110	13.64
Ela-Mana-Mou	Pitcairn	12	88	13.64
Darshaan	Shirley Heights	9	67	13.43

Form Sires

DAMSIRE - CONSISTENCY TABLE - AWT

DAMSIRE	DAMSIRE'S SIRE	WINS	RUNS	SR%
General Assembly	Secretariat	23	107	21.50
Mill Reef	Never Bend	31	158	19.62
Alzao	Lyphard	8	44	18.18
Red Alert	Red God	22	124	17.74
Secretariat	Bold Ruler	11	65	16.92
Ahonoora	Lorenzaccio	13	77	16.88
Blushing Groom	Red God	22	140	15.71
Caerleon	Nijinsky	14	90	15.56
High Top	Derring-Do	54	348	15.52
Top Ville	High Top	14	92	15.22
Pharly	Lyphard	13	86	15.12
Hot Spark	Habitat	11	74	14.86
Formidable	Forli	26	175	14.86
Nijinsky	Northern Dancer	24	163	14.72
Nonoalco	Nearctic	16	109	14.68
Irish River	Riverman	8	56	14.29
Reform	Pall Mall	21	151	13.91
Pas De Seul	Mill Reef	14	101	13.86
Vaguely Noble	Vienna	28	203	13.79
Green Dancer	Nijinsky	12	87	13.79
Dance In Time	Northern Dancer	24	175	13.71
Mount Hagen	Bold Bidder	10	73	13.70
Music Boy	Jukebox	33	252	13.10
Dominion	Derring-Do	29	223	13.00
Ballad Rock	Bold Lad (IRE)	11	85	12.94
Caro	Fortino II	18	140	12.86
Rarity	Hethersett	11	90	12.22
The Minstrel	Northern Dancer	9	75	12.00
Riverman	Never Bend	15	127	11.81
Star Appeal	Appiani II	25	224	11.16

70

Form Sires

SIRE	SIRE'S SIRE	OSR	RULE	IMP
Keen	Sharpen Up	7.53	16.16	2.15
Ballad Rock	Bold Lad (IRE)	6.98	13.68	1.96
Petorius	Mummy's Pet	8.46	15.20	1.80
Lugana Beach	Tumble Wind	10.51	18.89	1.80
Lear Fan	Roberto	13.68	23.08	1.69
Formidable	Forli	7.48	12.41	1.66
Most Welcome	Be My Guest	12.88	21.23	1.65
Polish Patriot	Danzig	12.19	20.00	1.64
Imperial Frontier	Lyphard	7.69	12.12	1.58
Soviet Lad	Nureyev	8.44	13.10	1.55
Nureyev	Northern Dancer	22.57	35.00	1.55
Primo Dominie	Dominion	9.58	14.55	1.52
Warrshan	Northern Baby	8.18	12.39	1.51
Distinctly North	Minshaanshu Amad	9.34	14.04	1.50
Ballacashtal	Vice Regent	8.09	12.12	1.50
Warning	Known Fact	13.47	20.17	1.50
Woodman	Mr Prospector	13.83	20.00	1.45
Rock City	Ballad Rock	9.77	14.08	1.44
Storm Cat	Storm Bird	17.96	25.53	1.42
Timeless Times	Timeless Moment	8.09	11.49	1.42
Don't Forget Me	Ahonoora	7.41	10.34	1.40
Forzando	Formidable	9.21	12.78	1.39
Damister	Mr Prospector	10.09	13.86	1.37
Petoski	Niniski	10.10	13.64	1.35
Beveled	Sharpen Up	9.60	12.93	1.35
Dowsing	Riverman	11.86	15.45	1.30
Risk Me	Sharpo	6.83	8.87	1.30
Be My Chief	Chief's Crown	9.80	12.64	1.29
Pennine Walk	Persian Bold	9.22	11.84	1.28
Superlative	Nebbiolo	9.16	11.76	1.28

Form Sires

DAMSIRE - IMPROVEMENT TABLE - AWT

DAMSIRE	DAMSIRE'S SIRE	OSR	RULE	IMP
General Assembly	Secretariat	12.17	21.50	1.77
Ballad Rock	Bold Lad (IRE)	7.79	12.94	1.66
Caerleon	Nijinsky	9.39	15.56	1.66
Formidable	Forli	9.04	14.86	1.64
Alzao	Lyphard	11.07	18.18	1.64
Nonoalco	Nearctic	8.98	14.68	1.63
Red Alert	Red God	11.31	17.74	1.57
Secretariat	Bold Ruler	10.96	16.92	1.54
Ahonoora	Lorenzaccio	11.00	16.88	1.53
Reform	Pall Mall	10.09	13.91	1.38
Hot Spark	Habitat	11.00	14.86	1.35
Music Boy	Jukebox	9.82	13.10	1.33
Pharly	Lyphard	11.58	15.12	1.31
Top Ville	High Top	11.69	15.22	1.30
Dominion	Derring-Do	10.09	13.00	1.29
Blushing Groom	Red God	12.30	15.71	1.28
High Top	Derring-Do	12.15	15.52	1.28
Sallust	Pall Mall	8.26	10.43	1.26
Dance In Time	Northern Dancer	10.86	13.71	1.26
Vaguely Noble	Vienna	11.17	13.79	1.23
Blakeney	Hethersett	8.13	10.00	1.23
Mill Reef	Never Bend	16.29	19.62	1.20
Pas De Seul	Mill Reef	11.51	13.86	1.20
Main Reef	Mill Reef	8.48	10.13	1.19
Star Appeal	Appiani II	9.44	11.16	1.18
Green Dancer	Nijinsky	12.00	13.79	1.15
Grundy	Great Nephew	8.96	10.26	1.14
Red Sunset	Red God	8.80	9.78	1.11
Song	Sing Sing	8.91	9.90	1.11
Welsh Pageant	Tudor Melody	10.19	11.07	1.09

Form Sires

Chapter 10

Performance Tables: Rest Pattern

SIRE - CONSISTENCY TABLE - REST PATTERN

SIRE	SIRE'S SIRE	WINS	RUNS	SR%
Red Ransom	Roberto	5	14	35.71
Dixieland Band	Northern Dancer	5	20	25.00
Storm Cat	Storm Bird	4	16	25.00
Nureyev	Northern Dancer	10	42	23.81
Danzig	Northern Dancer	12	53	22.64
Gone West	Mr Prospector	9	40	22.50
Sadler's Wells	Northern Dancer	30	134	22.39
Nashwan	Blushing Groom	13	59	22.03
Groom Dancer	Blushing Groom	6	28	21.43
Mr Prospector	Raise A Native	9	42	21.43
Polar Falcon	Nureyev	6	30	20.00
Warning	Known Fact	27	136	19.85
El Gran Senor	Northern Dancer	10	51	19.61
Machiavellian	Mr Prospector	7	36	19.44
Rainbow Quest	Blushing Groom	22	119	18.49
Darshaan	Shirley Heights	11	60	18.33
Dayjur	Danzig	6	33	18.18
Doyoun	Mill Reef	4	22	18.18
Zilzal	Nureyev	6	33	18.18
Danehill	Danzig	19	107	17.76
Rock City	Ballad Rock	15	85	17.65
Waajib	Try My Best	13	76	17.11
Alleged	Hoist The Flag	9	53	16.98
Diesis	Sharpen Up	12	72	16.67
Mtoto	Busted	12	72	16.67
Roi Danzig	Danzig	10	61	16.39
Imperial Frontier	Lyphard	5	33	15.15
Caerleon	Nijinsky	13	90	14.44
Most Welcome	Be My Guest	14	97	14.43
Ela-Mana-Mou	Pitcairn	9	63	14.29

Form Sires

DAMSIRE	DAMSIRE'S SIRE	WINS	RUNS	SR%
Fappiano	Mr Prospector	4	16	25.00
Teenoso	Youth	4	16	25.00
Exclusive Native	Raise A Native	6	28	21.43
Rousillon	Riverman	4	19	21.05
Topsider	Northern Dancer	6	30	20.00
Secreto	Northern Dancer	4	22	18.18
Lochnager	Dumbarnie	8	45	17.78
Nijinsky	Northern Dancer	21	120	17.50
Halo	Hail To Reason	6	35	17.14
The Minstrel	Northern Dancer	13	76	17.11
Roberto	Hail To Reason	10	61	16.39
Mount Hagen	Bold Bidder	6	37	16.22
Lomond	Northern Dancer	7	44	15.91
Mill Reef	Never Bend	20	126	15.87
Mr Prospector	Raise A Native	12	76	15.79
Kris	Sharpen Up	20	128	15.63
Night Shift	Northern Dancer	4	26	15.38
Thatching	Thatch	15	98	15.31
Affirmed	Exclusive Native	5	33	15.15
Northern Dancer	Nearctic	13	87	14.94
Sadler's Wells	Northern Dancer	7	47	14.89
High Top	Derring-Do	38	265	14.34
Danzig	Northern Dancer	6	43	13.95
Pharly	Lyphard	11	79	13.92
Top Ville	High Top	8	58	13.79
Busted	Crepello	17	130	13.08
Caerleon	Nijinsky	11	85	12.94
Niniski	Nijinsky	4	31	12.90
Storm Bird	Northern Dancer	4	31	12.90
Shareef Dancer	Northern Dancer	10	78	12.82

Form Sires

SIRE	SIRE'S SIRE	OSR	RULE	IMP
Waajib	Try My Best	7.98	17.11	2.14
Doyoun	Mill Reef	10.00	18.18	1.82
Dixieland Band	Northern Dancer	14.20	25.00	1.76
Groom Dancer	Blushing Groom	12.50	21.43	1.71
Roi Danzig	Danzig	10.00	16.39	1.64
Rock City	Ballad Rock	10.99	17.65	1.61
Weldnaas	Diesis	5.95	9.33	1.57
Common Grounds	Kris	9.01	14.14	1.57
Red Ransom	Roberto	23.17	35.71	1.54
Nashwan	Blushing Groom	14.33	22.03	1.54
Imperial Frontier	Lyphard	10.05	15.15	1.51
Keen	Sharpen Up	8.33	11.76	1.41
Tirol	Thatching	8.40	11.76	1.40
Darshaan	Shirley Heights	13.28	18.33	1.38
Polar Falcon	Nureyev	14.73	20.00	1.36
Riverman	Never Bend	10.02	13.33	1.33
Statoblest	Ahonoora	8.57	11.39	1.33
Warning	Known Fact	15.31	19.85	1.30
Danehill	Danzig	13.81	17.76	1.29
High Estate	Shirley Heights	10.28	13.21	1.29
Sadler's Wells	Northern Dancer	17.51	22.39	1.28
Rambo Dancer	Northern Dancer	8.14	10.34	1.27
Zilzal	Nureyev	14.34	18.18	1.27
Mtoto	Busted	13.20	16.67	1.26
Nureyev	Northern Dancer	18.86	23.81	1.26
El Gran Senor	Northern Dancer	15.61	19.61	1.26
Pennine Walk	Persian Bold	9.11	11.27	1.24
Damister	Mr Prospector	9.92	12.16	1.23
Emarati	Danzig	9.85	11.94	1.21
Petoski	Niniski	7.93	9.59	1.21
Last Tycoon	Try My Best	10.65	12.82	1.20
Salse	Topsider	11.88	14.29	1.20

Form Sires

<u>DAMSIRE - IMPROVEMENT TABLE - REST PATTERN</u>

DAMSIRE	DAMSIRE'S SIRE	OSR	RULE	IMP
Fappiano	Mr Prospector	14.49	25.00	1.73
Lochnager	Dumbarnie	10.43	17.78	1.70
Lomond	Northern Dancer	9.80	15.91	1.62
Ballad Rock	Bold Lad (IRE)	7.79	12.00	1.54
Thatching	Thatch	9.96	15.31	1.54
The Minstrel	Northern Dancer	11.37	17.11	1.50
Niniski	Nijinsky	9.13	12.90	1.41
Caerleon	Nijinsky	9.39	12.94	1.38
Halo	Hail To Reason	12.56	17.14	1.36
Kris	Sharpen Up	11.52	15.63	1.36
Rousillon	Riverman	15.83	21.05	1.33
Storm Bird	Northern Dancer	10.32	12.90	1.25
Red Sunset	Red God	8.80	10.91	1.24
Mr Prospector	Raise A Native	12.94	15.79	1.22
Busted	Crepello	10.74	13.08	1.22
Bustino	Busted	9.06	11.02	1.22
Nijinsky	Northern Dancer	14.40	17.50	1.22
Habat	Habitat	8.44	10.26	1.22
Bay Express	Polyfoto	9.24	11.11	1.20
Pharly	Lyphard	11.58	13.92	1.20
Dominion	Derring-Do	10.09	12.06	1.19
Lord Gayle	Sir Gaylord	7.68	9.17	1.19
High Top	Derring-Do	12.15	14.34	1.18
Top Ville	High Top	11.69	13.79	1.18
Topsider	Northern Dancer	17.21	20.00	1.16
Runnett	Mummy's Pet	7.73	8.77	1.13
Auction Ring	Bold Bidder	8.54	9.66	1.13
Roberto	Hail To Reason	14.50	16.39	1.13
Secreto	Northern Dancer	16.13	18.18	1.13
Luthier	Klairon	11.11	12.50	1.13

Form Sires

Chapter 11

Performance Tables: Track Type

SIRE - CONSISTENCY TABLE - STIFF

SIRE	SIRE'S SIRE	WINS	RUNS	SR%
Danzig	Northern Dancer	35	141	24.82
Generous	Caerleon	31	128	24.22
Gone West	Mr Prospector	22	101	21.78
Dayjur	Danzig	20	99	20.20
Mr Prospector	Raise A Native	22	120	18.33
Nashwan	Blushing Groom	34	186	18.28
Selkirk	Sharpen Up	14	80	17.50
Diesis	Sharpen Up	34	195	17.44
Zilzal	Nureyev	19	113	16.81
Shaadi	Danzig	26	155	16.77
Red Ransom	Roberto	12	72	16.67
Storm Cat	Storm Bird	10	60	16.67
Nureyev	Northern Dancer	22	133	16.54
Groom Dancer	Blushing Groom	14	85	16.47
Bering	Arctic Tern	18	110	16.36
Machiavellian	Mr Prospector	23	141	16.31
El Gran Senor	Northern Dancer	18	113	15.93
Sadler's Wells	Northern Dancer	68	430	15.81
Saddlers' Hall	Sadler's Wells	9	57	15.79
Ela-Mana-Mou	Pitcairn	25	162	15.43
Alleged	Hoist The Flag	18	117	15.38
Caerleon	Nijinsky	42	278	15.11
Green Dancer	Nijinsky	12	80	15.00
Polish Precedent	Danzig	24	160	15.00
Elmaamul	Diesis	15	103	14.56
Kris	Sharpen Up	41	282	14.54
Royal Academy	Nijinsky	33	232	14.22
Polish Patriot	Danzig	24	171	14.04
Irish River	Riverman	9	65	13.85
Old Vic	Sadler's Wells	18	130	13.85

Form Sires

SIRE	SIRE'S SIRE	OSR	RULE	IMP
Soviet Lad	Nureyev	7.12	11.49	1.61
Saddlers' Hall	Sadler's Wells	9.80	15.79	1.61
Shalford	Thatching	7.03	10.68	1.52
Salt Dome	Blushing Groom	8.23	11.28	1.37
Lugana Beach	Tumble Wind	7.63	10.38	1.36
Gone West	Mr Prospector	16.67	21.78	1.31
Be My Guest	Northern Dancer	10.29	13.27	1.29
Tirol	Thatching	9.12	11.59	1.27
Archway	Thatching	8.19	10.39	1.27
Polish Patriot	Danzig	11.07	14.04	1.27
Forzando	Formidable	8.27	10.12	1.22
Common Grounds	Kris	9.28	11.30	1.22
Elmaamul	Diesis	12.00	14.56	1.21
Waajib	Try My Best	8.93	10.81	1.21
Warrshan	Northern Dancer	6.87	8.26	1.20
Danzig	Northern Dancer	20.81	24.82	1.19
Generous	Caerleon	20.30	24.22	1.19
Safawan	Young Generation	9.73	11.49	1.18
Shaadi	Danzig	14.23	16.77	1.18
Bering	Arctic Tern	13.97	16.36	1.17
Kris	Sharpen Up	12.42	14.54	1.17
Ballacashtal	Vice Regent	6.57	7.56	1.15
Groom Dancer	Blushing Groom	14.34	16.47	1.15
Puissance	Thatching	8.62	9.80	1.14
Diesis	Sharpen Up	15.40	17.44	1.13
Old Vic	Sadler's Wells	12.26	13.85	1.13
Cyrano De Bergerac	Bold Lad (IRE)	7.29	8.19	1.12
Bairn	Northern Baby	8.78	9.83	1.12
Mujadil	Storm Bird	11.02	12.24	1.11
Polish Precedent	Danzig	13.50	15.00	1.11

Form Sires

SIRE	SIRE'S SIRE	WINS	RUNS	SR%
Nureyev	Northern Dancer	16	45	35.56
Dashing Blade	Elegant Air	9	33	27.27
Danzig	Northern Dancer	13	48	27.08
Dayjur	Danzig	10	43	23.26
Sadler's Wells	Northern Dancer	31	158	19.62
Storm Cat	Storm Bird	8	41	19.51
Rainbow Quest	Blushing Groom	20	105	19.05
Polar Falcon	Nureyev	14	74	18.92
El Gran Senor	Northern Dancer	15	80	18.75
Soviet Star	Nureyev	20	109	18.35
Shavian	Kris	15	82	18.29
Sayf El Arab	Drone	12	68	17.65
Generous	Caerleon	7	41	17.07
Distant Relative	Habitat	24	141	17.02
In The Wings	Sadler's Wells	9	53	16.98
Caerleon	Nijinsky	19	112	16.96
Ela-Mana-Mou	Pitcairn	11	68	16.18
Machiavellian	Mr Prospector	8	51	15.69
Green Desert	Danzig	36	232	15.52
Cadeaux Genereux	Young Generation	29	188	15.43
Zilzal	Nureyev	9	59	15.25
Kefaah	Blushing Groom	11	73	15.07
Known Fact	In Reality	11	73	15.07
Lear Fan	Roberto	10	67	14.93
Mujadil	Storm Bird	10	67	14.93
Imp Society	Barrera	10	68	14.71
Persian Bold	Bold Lad (IRE)	24	164	14.63
Tirol	Thatching	17	117	14.53
Unfuwain	Northern Dancer	16	111	14.41
Petoski	Niniski	13	92	14.13

Form Sires

SIRE - IMPROVEMENT TABLE - EASY

SIRE	SIRE'S SIRE	OSR	RULE	IMP
Dashing Blade	Elegant Air	13.16	27.27	2.07
Imp Society	Barrera	8.36	14.71	1.76
Batshoof	Sadler's Wells	7.86	13.79	1.75
Nureyev	Northern Dancer	21.43	35.56	1.66
Tirol	Thatching	9.12	14.53	1.59
Ballad Rock	Bold Lad (IRE)	6.13	9.76	1.59
Shareef Dancer	Northern Dancer	6.80	10.65	1.57
Nordico	Northern Dancer	8.22	12.87	1.57
Petoski	Niniski	9.14	14.13	1.55
Distinctly North	Minshaanshu Amad	8.75	13.25	1.51
Sayf El Arab	Drone	11.73	17.65	1.50
Nomination	Dominion	7.78	11.57	1.49
Weldnaas	Diesis	5.72	8.23	1.44
Kefaah	Blushing Groom	10.86	15.07	1.39
Sharpo	Sharpen Up	9.74	13.46	1.38
Fayruz	Song	8.35	11.54	1.38
Distant Relative	Habitat	12.46	17.02	1.37
Mujadil	Storm Bird	11.02	14.93	1.35
Risk Me	Sharpo	6.42	8.55	1.33
Rainbow Quest	Blushing Groom	14.36	19.05	1.33
Never So Bold	Bold Lad (IRE)	8.02	10.50	1.31
Warrshan	Northern Dancer	6.87	8.99	1.31
Danzig	Northern Dancer	20.81	27.08	1.30
Komaite	Nureyev	8.46	11.00	1.30
Shavian	Kris	14.15	18.29	1.29
Interrex	Vice Regent	8.00	10.28	1.29
Dowsing	Riverman	10.99	14.04	1.28
Pennine Walk	Persian Bold	8.23	10.47	1.27
Last Tycoon	Try My Best	11.12	14.11	1.27
Try My Best	Northern Dancer	10.08	12.68	1.26

Form Sires

SIRE	SIRE'S SIRE	WINS	RUNS	SR%
Machiavellian	Mr Prospector	15	70	21.43
In The Wings	Sadler's Wells	15	72	20.83
Dayjur	Danzig	11	53	20.75
Nureyev	Northern Dancer	13	64	20.31
Sadler's Wells	Northern Dancer	48	241	19.92
Generous	Caerleon	14	71	19.72
Zilzal	Nureyev	16	82	19.51
Alleged	Hoist The Flag	10	53	18.87
El Gran Senor	Northern Dancer	18	97	18.56
Cadeaux Genereux	Young Generation	43	237	18.14
Known Fact	In Reality	12	69	17.39
Mr Prospector	Raise A Native	9	52	17.31
Polar Falcon	Nureyev	16	93	17.20
Soviet Star	Nureyev	24	140	17.14
Lycius	Mr Prospector	14	82	17.07
Caerleon	Nijinsky	28	166	16.87
Danzig	Northern Dancer	12	73	16.44
Archway	Thatching	10	61	16.39
Green Desert	Danzig	56	347	16.14
Shavian	Kris	14	88	15.91
Sayf El Arab	Drone	17	107	15.89
Safawan	Young Generation	11	71	15.49
Rainbow Quest	Blushing Groom	27	176	15.34
Dowsing	Riverman	46	303	15.18
Rousillon	Riverman	20	132	15.15
Ela-Mana-Mou	Pitcairn	16	109	14.68
Shirley Heights	Mill Reef	25	177	14.12
Danehill	Danzig	39	277	14.08
Statoblest	Ahonoora	38	270	14.07
Sharrood	Caro	22	157	14.01

Form Sires

SIRE - IMPROVEMENT TABLE - SHARP

SIRE	SIRE'S SIRE	OSR	RULE	IMP
Archway	Thatching	8.19	16.39	2.00
Safawan	Young Generation	9.73	15.49	1.59
Imp Society	Barrera	8.36	12.94	1.55
Lycius	Mr Prospector	11.37	17.07	1.50
Batshoof	Sadler's Wells	7.86	11.49	1.46
Komaite	Nureyev	8.46	12.23	1.45
Lugana Beach	Tumble Wind	7.63	10.98	1.44
Treasure Kay	Mummy's Pet	9.65	13.84	1.43
Interrex	Vice Regent	8.00	11.11	1.39
In The Wings	Sadler's Wells	15.01	20.83	1.39
Dowsing	Riverman	10.99	15.18	1.38
Puissance	Thatching	8.62	11.76	1.37
Bairn	Northern Baby	8.78	11.93	1.36
Sayf El Arab	Drone	11.73	15.89	1.35
Statoblest	Ahonoora	10.40	14.07	1.35
Superlative	Nebbiolo	8.42	11.17	1.33
Keen	Sharpen Up	5.01	6.60	1.32
Petoski	Niniski	9.14	11.94	1.31
Distinctly North	Minshaanshu Amad	8.75	11.37	1.30
Formidable	Forli	5.48	6.98	1.27
Doulab	Topsider	8.65	10.99	1.27
Known Fact	In Reality	13.71	17.39	1.27
Cyrano De Bergerac	Bold Lad (IRE)	7.29	9.18	1.26
Hadeer	General Assembly	6.93	8.67	1.25
Cadeaux Genereux	Young Generation	14.53	18.14	1.25
Clantime	Music Boy	9.95	12.24	1.23
Green Desert	Danzig	13.13	16.14	1.23
Tirol	Thatching	9.12	11.18	1.23
Machiavellian	Mr Prospector	17.48	21.43	1.23
Riverman	Never Bend	10.78	13.04	1.21

Form Sires

SIRE	SIRE'S SIRE	WINS	RUNS	SR%
Mr Prospector	Raise A Native	33	138	23.91
Generous	Caerleon	38	185	20.54
Storm Cat	Storm Bird	14	76	18.42
Danzig	Northern Dancer	38	209	18.18
Nashwan	Blushing Groom	44	246	17.89
Dayjur	Danzig	25	142	17.61
Red Ransom	Roberto	16	92	17.39
Dixieland Band	Northern Dancer	14	85	16.47
Selkirk	Sharpen Up	19	116	16.38
Diesis	Sharpen Up	47	287	16.38
Nureyev	Northern Dancer	30	184	16.30
Sadler's Wells	Northern Dancer	99	618	16.02
Caerleon	Nijinsky	61	390	15.64
Gone West	Mr Prospector	24	154	15.58
Zilzal	Nureyev	22	144	15.28
Silver Hawk	Roberto	36	236	15.25
Machiavellian	Mr Prospector	27	182	14.84
Alleged	Hoist The Flag	27	182	14.84
Bering	Arctic Tern	23	162	14.20
Elmaamul	Diesis	17	120	14.17
Lear Fan	Roberto	30	216	13.89
Polar Falcon	Nureyev	28	202	13.86
Danehill	Danzig	78	563	13.85
Green Dancer	Nijinsky	13	95	13.68
Ela-Mana-Mou	Pitcairn	27	198	13.64
Cadeaux Genereux	Young Generation	72	529	13.61
Tragic Role	Nureyev	17	126	13.49
Lahib	Riverman	9	67	13.43
Soviet Star	Nureyev	37	278	13.31
Kris	Sharpen Up	48	362	13.26

Form Sires

SIRE - IMPROVEMENT TABLE - GALLOPING

SIRE	SIRE'S SIRE	OSR	RULE	IMP
Imperial Frontier	Lyphard	6.58	8.54	1.30
Lahib	Riverman	10.75	13.43	1.25
Treasure Kay	Mummy's Pet	9.65	11.45	1.19
Saddlers' Hall	Sadler's Wells	9.80	11.59	1.18
Elmaamul	Diesis	12.00	14.17	1.18
Damister	Mr Prospector	9.28	10.94	1.18
Silver Hawk	Roberto	13.09	15.25	1.17
Timeless Times	Timeless Moment	6.95	7.94	1.14
Storm Cat	Storm Bird	16.16	18.42	1.14
Marju	Last Tycoon	11.28	12.42	1.10
Archway	Thatching	8.19	8.97	1.10
Lear Fan	Roberto	12.68	13.89	1.10
Salse	Topsider	12.14	13.19	1.09
Waajib	Try My Best	8.93	9.70	1.09
Mazilier	Lyphard	8.97	9.70	1.08
High Estate	Shirley Heights	10.23	10.99	1.07
Kris	Sharpen Up	12.42	13.26	1.07
Diesis	Sharpen Up	15.40	16.38	1.06
Nashwan	Blushing Groom	16.82	17.89	1.06
Mr Prospector	Raise A Native	22.55	23.91	1.06
Ballad Rock	Bold Lad (IRE)	6.13	6.44	1.05
Rudimentary	Nureyev	7.35	7.69	1.05
Bluebird	Storm Bird	11.48	12.01	1.05
Dominion	Derring-Do	9.97	10.42	1.04
Shalford	Thatching	7.03	7.32	1.04
Pharly	Lyphard	10.60	11.01	1.04
Pennine Walk	Persian Bold	8.23	8.46	1.03
Interrex	Vice Regent	8.00	8.21	1.03
Petorius	Mummy's Pet	7.18	7.36	1.02
Bering	Arctic Tern	13.97	14.20	1.02

Form Sires

SIRE	SIRE'S SIRE	WINS	RUNS	SR%
Mr Prospector	Raise A Native	10	44	22.73
In The Wings	Sadler's Wells	16	72	22.22
Selkirk	Sharpen Up	8	36	22.22
El Gran Senor	Northern Dancer	17	77	22.08
Generous	Caerleon	13	59	22.03
Danzig	Northern Dancer	14	64	21.88
Machiavellian	Mr Prospector	14	67	20.90
Polar Falcon	Nureyev	20	100	20.00
Unfuwain	Northern Dancer	27	143	18.88
Cadeaux Genereux	Young Generation	41	227	18.06
Rousillon	Riverman	21	117	17.95
Soviet Star	Nureyev	19	106	17.92
Gone West	Mr Prospector	9	51	17.65
Archway	Thatching	9	52	17.31
Ela-Mana-Mou	Pitcairn	21	123	17.07
Green Desert	Danzig	50	293	17.06
Kahyasi	Ile De Bourbon	8	47	17.02
Polish Patriot	Danzig	24	142	16.90
Caerleon	Nijinsky	25	148	16.89
Sadler's Wells	Northern Dancer	32	192	16.67
Dayjur	Danzig	8	48	16.67
Slip Anchor	Shirley Heights	31	189	16.40
Groom Dancer	Blushing Groom	9	55	16.36
Royal Academy	Nijinsky	25	155	16.13
Sayf El Arab	Drone	17	106	16.04
Lycius	Mr Prospector	14	88	15.91
Riverman	Never Bend	13	82	15.85
Nureyev	Northern Dancer	9	57	15.79
Red Sunset	Red God	23	148	15.54
Nashwan	Blushing Groom	13	88	14.77

Form Sires

SIRE - IMPROVEMENT TABLE - UNDULATING

SIRE	SIRE'S SIRE	OSR	RULE	IMP
Archway	Thatching	8.19	17.31	2.11
Warrshan	Northern Dancer	6.87	11.34	1.65
Kahyasi	Ile De Bourbon	10.65	17.02	1.60
Red Sunset	Red God	9.73	15.54	1.60
Tirol	Thatching	9.12	13.92	1.53
Polish Patriot	Danzig	11.07	16.90	1.53
In The Wings	Sadler's Wells	15.01	22.22	1.48
Riverman	Never Bend	10.78	15.85	1.47
Rock City	Ballad Rock	8.82	12.90	1.46
Distinctly North	Minshaanshu Amad	8.75	12.64	1.44
Ballad Rock	Bold Lad (IRE)	6.13	8.85	1.44
Unfuwain	Northern Dancer	13.43	18.88	1.41
Lycius	Mr Prospector	11.37	15.91	1.40
Sayf El Arab	Drone	11.73	16.04	1.37
El Gran Senor	Northern Dancer	16.19	22.08	1.36
Rousillon	Riverman	13.28	17.95	1.35
Imp Society	Barrera	8.36	11.24	1.34
Safawan	Young Generation	9.73	13.04	1.34
Night Shift	Northern Dancer	11.06	14.74	1.33
Polar Falcon	Nureyev	15.12	20.00	1.32
Pennine Walk	Persian Bold	8.23	10.71	1.30
Green Desert	Danzig	13.13	17.06	1.30
Lugana Beach	Tumble Wind	7.63	9.89	1.30
Slip Anchor	Shirley Heights	12.68	16.40	1.29
Superlative	Nebbiolo	8.42	10.88	1.29
Tina's Pet	Mummy's Pet	7.36	9.41	1.28
Last Tycoon	Try My Best	11.12	14.01	1.26
Cadeaux Genereux	Young Generation	14.53	18.06	1.24
Clantime	Music Boy	9.95	12.31	1.24
Kefaah	Blushing Groom	10.86	13.41	1.24

Form Sires

Chapter 12

Performance Tables: Handicaps

<u>SIRE - CONSISTENCY TABLE - HANDICAP</u>

SIRE	SIRE'S SIRE	WINS	RUNS	SR%
Danzig	Northern Dancer	30	167	17.96
Mr Prospector	Raise A Native	10	58	17.24
Storm Cat	Storm Bird	16	96	16.67
Arazi	Blushing Groom	7	42	16.67
Generous	Caerleon	18	112	16.07
Dayjur	Danzig	13	82	15.85
Dashing Blade	Elegant Air	18	123	14.63
Dixieland Band	Northern Dancer	20	137	14.60
Sadler's Wells	Northern Dancer	59	407	14.50
Doyoun	Mill Reef	13	90	14.44
Great Commotion	Nureyev	8	56	14.29
Nureyev	Northern Dancer	16	120	13.33
Caerleon	Nijinsky	58	446	13.00
In The Wings	Sadler's Wells	26	200	13.00
Zilzal	Nureyev	13	103	12.62
Kefaah	Blushing Groom	30	238	12.61
Lear Fan	Roberto	33	265	12.45
Mystiko	Secreto	11	90	12.22
Shirley Heights	Mill Reef	50	411	12.17
Sayf El Arab	Drone	41	338	12.13
Komaite	Nureyev	63	521	12.09
Green Dancer	Nijinsky	12	100	12.00
Rainbow Quest	Blushing Groom	60	501	11.98
Cadeaux Genereux	Young Generation	77	643	11.98
Tragic Role	Nureyev	20	168	11.90
Ela-Mana-Mou	Pitcairn	39	328	11.89
Kalaglow	Kalamoun	40	340	11.76
Soviet Star	Nureyev	36	306	11.76
Unfuwain	Northern Dancer	36	307	11.73
Most Welcome	Be My Guest	71	608	11.68

Form Sires

SIRE	SIRE'S SIRE	OSR	RULE	IMP
Mystiko	Secreto	6.97	12.22	1.75
Shalford	Thatching	7.58	10.71	1.41
Arazi	Blushing Groom	12.90	16.67	1.29
Kefaah	Blushing Groom	10.86	12.61	1.16
Imperial Frontier	Lyphard	7.69	8.90	1.16
Ballacashtal	Vice Regent	8.09	9.30	1.15
Superlative	Nebbiolo	9.16	10.24	1.12
Dashing Blade	Elegant Air	13.10	14.63	1.12
Interrex	Vice Regent	8.43	9.24	1.10
Rambo Dancer	Northern Dancer	8.29	9.01	1.09
Clantime	Music Boy	9.30	10.10	1.09
Bairn	Northern Baby	9.08	9.86	1.09
Tina's Pet	Mummy's Pet	7.42	8.06	1.09
Sayf El Arab	Drone	11.37	12.13	1.07
Shareef Dancer	Northern Dancer	6.17	6.58	1.07
Never So Bold	Bold Lad (IRE)	7.55	7.95	1.05
Pennine Walk	Persian Bold	9.22	9.69	1.05
Komaite	Nureyev	11.76	12.09	1.03
Weldnaas	Diesis	6.19	6.36	1.03
Nomination	Dominion	7.37	7.54	1.02
Roi Danzig	Danzig	10.62	10.81	1.02
Damister	Mr Prospector	10.09	10.26	1.02
Safawan	Young Generation	9.70	9.86	1.02
Persian Bold	Bold Lad (IRE)	11.43	11.57	1.01
Cyrano De Bergerac	Bold Lad (IRE)	7.54	7.57	1.00
Petorius	Mummy's Pet	8.46	8.46	1.00
Petoski	Niniski	10.10	10.09	1.00
Archway	Thatching	8.43	8.40	1.00

Form Sires

SIRE	SIRE'S SIRE	WNRS	WINS	RATIO
Dashing Blade	Elegant Air	4	18	4.50
Sayf El Arab	Drone	11	41	3.73
Interrex	Vice Regent	7	22	3.14
Bering	Arctic Tern	7	22	3.14
Kalaglow	Kalamoun	13	40	3.08
Doulab	Topsider	20	60	3.00
Superlative	Nebbiolo	17	46	2.71
Dowsing	Riverman	27	73	2.70
Ballacashtal	Vice Regent	12	32	2.67
Storm Cat	Storm Bird	6	16	2.67
Komaite	Nureyev	24	63	2.63
Pharly	Lyphard	20	52	2.60
Primo Dominie	Dominion	32	83	2.59
Shareef Dancer	Northern Dancer	12	31	2.58
Bairn	Northern Baby	19	49	2.58
Try My Best	Northern Dancer	11	28	2.55
Pennine Walk	Persian Bold	15	38	2.53
Kefaah	Blushing Groom	12	30	2.50
Treasure Kay	Mummy's Pet	13	32	2.46
Shaadi	Danzig	13	32	2.46
Weldnaas	Diesis	9	22	2.44
Hadeer	General Assembly	14	34	2.43
Clantime	Music Boy	32	77	2.41
Safawan	Young Generation	6	14	2.33
Efisio	Formidable	48	112	2.33
Danzig	Northern Dancer	13	30	2.31
Petoski	Niniski	14	32	2.29
Aragon	Mummy's Pet	25	57	2.28
Cadeaux Genereux	Young Generation	34	77	2.26
Last Tycoon	Try My Best	23	52	2.26

Mystiko features at the top of the HandicapImprovement table (p. 88)

Form Sires

Chapter 13

Form Factor Analysis - Negative Results

This chapter lists all sires and damsires who performed poorly during analysis of the major form factors. I have concentrated on the 'improvement tables' as these show the deterioration in performance most graphically. Only sires and damsires who achieve a performance rating of 0.70 or less qualify for the lists. The three columns represent the overall strike rate (OSR), the strike rate under rule (RULE), and the resulting performance rating, which are negative (NEG) as they are less than 1.

I have not covered 'distances' in this section as obviously those horses who are sprinters will be unlikely to stay - and those horses who are stayers will score poorly over sprint trips.

The lists should prove very informative from a punting point of view, as they will enable the horseplayer to avoid the progeny of sires and damsires who are likely to be heavily disadvantaged by certain conditions. Should such animals be well supported in the market, maybe even to favouritism, then this could also offer the prospect of value odds on the other runners.

RATE OF MATURITY

Sire - Age (2)

SIRE	SIRE'S SIRE	OSR	RULE	NEG
Bairn	Northern Baby	9.08	1.79	0.20
Mystiko	Secreto	6.97	1.69	0.24
Pennine Walk	Persian Bold	9.22	2.56	0.28
Old Vic	Sadler's Wells	11.74	3.92	0.33
Broken Hearted	Dara Monarch	11.63	6.25	0.54
Kefaah	Blushing Groom	10.86	6.25	0.58
Be My Guest	Northern Dancer	10.69	6.62	0.62
Never So Bold	Bold Lad (IRE)	7.55	4.93	0.65
Alleged	Hoist The Flag	17.86	11.76	0.66
Safawan	Young Generation	9.70	6.49	0.67
Dominion	Derring-Do	10.07	6.76	0.67
Interrex	Vice Regent	8.43	5.83	0.69

Form Sires

Damsire - Age (2)

DAMSIRE	DAMSIRE'S SIRE	OSR	RULE	NEG
Reform	Pall Mall	10.09	3.96	0.39
Troy	Petingo	11.56	4.76	0.41
Caro	Fortino II	12.62	6.15	0.49
Alleged	Hoist The Flag	9.45	4.76	0.50
Great Nephew	Honeyway	8.74	4.71	0.54
General Assembly	Secretariat	12.17	7.32	0.60
Habat	Habitat	8.44	5.66	0.67
Formidable	Forli	9.04	6.13	0.68
Teenoso	Youth	23.80	16.67	0.70

Sire - Age (3)

DAMSIRE	SIRE'S SIRE	OSR	RULE	NEG
Try My Best	Northern Dancer	9.51	4.26	0.45
Tina's Pet	Mummy's Pet	7.42	3.57	0.48
Interrex	Vice Regent	8.43	4.58	0.54
Tragic Role	Nureyev	12.89	7.38	0.57
Hadeer	General Assembly	6.89	4.01	0.58
Lycius	Mr Prospector	10.51	6.64	0.63
Great Commotion	Nureyev	16.38	10.53	0.64
Kalaglow	Kalamoun	13.39	8.84	0.66
Lugana Beach	Tumble Wind	10.51	7.09	0.67
Ballacashtal	Vice Regent	8.09	5.47	0.68
Aragon	Mummy's Pet	8.12	5.50	0.68
Known Fact	In Reality	12.80	8.79	0.69

Damsire - Age (3)

DAMSIRE	DAMSIRE'S SIRE	OSR	RULE	NEG
Bay Express	Polyfoto	9.24	3.63	0.39
Try My Best	Northern Dancer	8.38	4.68	0.56
Rainbow Quest	Blushing Groom	14.40	8.33	0.58
Dance In Time	Northern Dancer	10.86	6.36	0.59
Rarity	Hethersett	13.71	9.35	0.68
Mummy's Pet	Sing Sing	8.06	5.65	0.70

Form Sires

GOING

DAMSIRE	SIRE'S SIRE	OSR	RULE	NEG
Keen	Sharpen Up	7.53	0.00	0.00
Formidable	Forli	7.48	2.00	0.27
Pursuit Of Love	Groom Dancer	10.97	3.70	0.34
Superlative	Nebbiolo	9.16	3.67	0.40
Ballad Rock	Bold Lad (IRE)	6.98	2.88	0.41
Gone West	Mr Prospector	16.62	6.98	0.42
Imp Society	Barrera	8.91	3.90	0.44
Rock City	Ballad Rock	9.77	4.63	0.47
Kahyasi	Ile De Bourbon	11.26	5.49	0.49
Pharly	Lyphard	10.57	5.19	0.49
Batshoof	Sadler's Wells	8.70	4.48	0.51
Timeless Times	Timeless Moment	8.09	4.17	0.52
Weldnaas	Diesis	6.19	3.19	0.52
Clantime	Music Boy	9.30	5.15	0.55
Puissance	Thatching	8.45	4.80	0.57
Reprimand	Mummy's Pet	9.14	5.23	0.57
Dashing Blade	Elegant Air	13.10	7.50	0.57
Mystiko	Secreto	6.97	4.00	0.57
Kefaah	Blushing Groom	10.86	6.25	0.58
Sayf El Arab	Drone	11.37	6.82	0.60
Petoski	Niniski	10.10	6.17	0.61
Arazi	Blushing Groom	12.90	8.00	0.62
Dayjur	Danzig	19.13	11.90	0.62
Priolo	Sovereign Dancer	13.09	8.20	0.63
Lear Fan	Roberto	13.68	8.60	0.63
Silver Hawk	Roberto	13.58	8.60	0.63
Polish Precedent	Danzig	13.48	8.91	0.66
Pennine Walk	Persian Bold	9.22	6.19	0.67
Petorius	Mummy's Pet	8.46	5.77	0.68
Caerleon	Nijinsky	15.97	11.02	0.69

Form Sires

Damsire - Going (Soft)

DAMSIRE	DAMSIRE'S SIRE	OSR	RULE	NEG
Ballad Rock	Bold Lad (IRE)	7.79	1.52	0.19
Roberto	Hail To Reason	14.50	4.55	0.31
Caerleon	Nijinsky	9.39	3.00	0.32
Secretariat	Bold Ruler	10.96	4.35	0.40
Storm Bird	Northern Dancer	10.32	4.65	0.45
Vaguely Noble	Vienna	11.17	5.84	0.52
Fappiano	Mr Prospector	14.49	7.69	0.53
Formidable	Forli	9.04	5.00	0.55
Red Alert	Red God	11.31	6.42	0.57
Luthier	Klairon	11.11	6.35	0.57
Habat	Habitat	8.44	4.88	0.58
Reform	Pall Mall	10.09	5.97	0.59
Nureyev	Northern Dancer	11.52	6.98	0.61
Frimley Park	Tribal Chief	11.27	6.90	0.61
Seattle Slew	Bold Reasoning	12.57	7.69	0.61
Troy	Petingo	11.56	7.14	0.62
Topsider	Northern Dancer	17.21	10.71	0.62
Bellypha	Lyphard	13.31	8.33	0.63
Persian Bold	Bold Lad (IRE)	10.93	6.88	0.63
Bustino	Busted	9.06	5.88	0.65
Kings Lake	Nijinsky	9.40	6.15	0.65
Nijinsky	Northern Dancer	14.40	9.48	0.66
Sadler's Wells	Northern Dancer	16.46	10.87	0.66
Hot Spark	Habitat	11.00	7.50	0.68
Lyphard	Northern Dancer	13.68	9.45	0.69
Try My Best	Northern Dancer	8.38	5.80	0.69
Kalaglow	Kalamoun	12.54	8.70	0.69
Ile De Bourbon	Nijinsky	11.69	8.16	0.70

Sire - Going (Firm)

Doyoun	Mill Reef	15.94	7.89	0.50
Lugana Beach	Tumble Wind	10.51	5.26	0.50
Imperial Frontier	Lyphard	7.69	4.10	0.53
Komaite	Nureyev	11.76	6.98	0.59
Marju	Last Tycoon	11.58	7.98	0.69

Damsire - Going (Firm)

Key To The Mint	Graustark	13.74	8.93	0.65
Majestic Light	Majestic Prince	17.89	11.76	0.66

94

Form Sires

WEIGHT

Sire - Weight

DAMSIRE	SIRE'S SIRE	OSR	RULE	NEG
Red Ransom	Roberto	18.28	0.00	0.00
Rudimentary	Nureyev	7.55	0.00	0.00
Soviet Lad	Nureyev	8.44	0.00	0.00
Silver Hawk	Roberto	13.58	1.89	0.14
Tirol	Thatching	8.81	1.89	0.21
Nomination	Dominion	7.37	1.75	0.24
Groom Dancer	Blushing Groom	13.84	5.71	0.41
Gone West	Mr Prospector	16.62	7.14	0.43
Irish River	Riverman	11.28	5.00	0.44
Diesis	Sharpen Up	15.05	7.58	0.50
Machiavellian	Mr Prospector	17.87	9.38	0.52
Shavian	Kris	12.79	7.14	0.56
Elmaamul	Diesis	11.72	6.90	0.59
Archway	Thatching	8.43	5.00	0.59
Primo Dominie	Dominion	9.58	5.78	0.60
Marju	Last Tycoon	11.58	7.14	0.62
Riverman	Never Bend	10.63	6.56	0.62
Sharpo	Sharpen Up	9.94	6.18	0.62
Common Grounds	Kris	9.01	5.62	0.62
Mr Prospector	Raise A Native	22.30	14.29	0.64
Polar Falcon	Nureyev	15.14	10.34	0.68
Pursuit Of Love	Groom Dancer	10.97	7.69	0.70

Damsire - Weight

DAMSIRE	DAMSIRE'S SIRE	OSR	RULE	NEG
Halo	Hail To Reason	12.56	0.00	0.00
Lomond	Northern Dancer	9.80	0.00	0.00
Storm Bird	Northern Dancer	10.32	0.00	0.00
Alleged	Hoist The Flag	9.45	2.44	0.26
Nureyev	Northern Dancer	11.52	3.85	0.33
Ela-Mana-Mou	Pitcairn	10.50	3.85	0.37
Nebbiolo	Yellow God	11.92	4.44	0.37
Red Sunset	Red God	8.80	3.85	0.44
Indian King	Raja Baba	10.28	4.55	0.44
Frimley Park	Tribal Chief	11.27	5.26	0.47

Form Sires

Auction Ring	Bold Bidder	8.54	4.21	0.49
Runnett	Mummy's Pet	7.73	4.35	0.56
Mummy's Pet	Sing Sing	8.06	4.93	0.61
Kris	Sharpen Up	11.52	7.14	0.62
Northern Dancer	Nearctic	15.30	9.68	0.63
Relkino	Relko	9.64	6.15	0.64
The Minstrel	Northern Dancer	11.37	7.69	0.68
Known Fact	In Reality	10.56	7.27	0.69
Riverman	Never Bend	13.44	9.41	0.70

ALL-WEATHER
Sire - All-Weather

DAMSIRE	SIRE'S SIRE	OSR	RULE	NEG
Irish River	Riverman	11.28	0.00	0.00
Lycius	Mr Prospector	10.51	2.44	0.23
Nashwan	Blushing Groom	16.31	4.35	0.27
Broken Hearted	Dara Monarch	11.63	3.33	0.29
Shareef Dancer	Northern Dancer	6.17	1.85	0.30
Green Dancer	Nijinsky	15.06	5.26	0.35
Bering	Arctic Tern	12.96	4.55	0.35
Emarati	Danzig	9.51	4.13	0.43
Waajib	Try My Best	8.31	3.74	0.45
Statoblest	Ahonoora	9.72	4.50	0.46
Shavian	Kris	12.79	6.15	0.48
Try My Best	Northern Dancer	9.51	4.65	0.49
Clantime	Music Boy	9.30	4.91	0.53
Soviet Star	Nureyev	14.41	7.81	0.54
Alleged	Hoist The Flag	17.86	10.00	0.56
Never So Bold	Bold Lad (IRE)	7.55	4.31	0.57
Known Fact	In Reality	12.80	7.32	0.57
Persian Bold	Bold Lad (IRE)	11.43	6.60	0.58
Salt Dome	Blushing Groom	7.76	4.49	0.58
Old Vic	Sadler's Wells	11.74	6.82	0.58
Diesis	Sharpen Up	15.05	8.82	0.59
Tragic Role	Nureyev	12.89	7.58	0.59
Sadler's Wells	Northern Dancer	18.66	11.11	0.60
El Gran Senor	Northern Dancer	15.40	9.68	0.63
Distant Relative	Habitat	11.68	7.38	0.63
Slip Anchor	Shirley Heights	12.14	7.77	0.64
In The Wings	Sadler's Wells	14.62	9.38	0.64
Tirol	Thatching	8.81	5.71	0.65
Fairy King	Northern Dancer	13.13	8.82	0.67

Form Sires

Damsire - All-Weather

DAMSIRE	DAMSIRE'S SIRE	OSR	RULE	NEG
Frimley Park	Tribal Chief	11.27	0.00	0.00
Northern Dancer	Nearctic	15.30	2.38	0.16
Nebbiolo	Yellow God	11.92	2.27	0.19
Darshaan	Shirley Heights	14.73	4.35	0.30
Mummy's Pet	Sing Sing	8.06	3.27	0.41
Lyphard	Northern Dancer	13.68	6.67	0.49
Roberto	Hail To Reason	14.50	8.16	0.56
Alleged	Hoist The Flag	9.45	5.38	0.57
Habat	Habitat	8.44	5.08	0.60
Shareef Dancer	Northern Dancer	13.72	8.33	0.61
Lord Gayle	Sir Gaylord	7.68	4.81	0.63
Northfields	Northern Dancer	10.93	7.27	0.67

REST-PATTERN

Sire - Rest-Pattern

DAMSIRE	SIRE'S SIRE	OSR	RULE	NEG
Anshan	Persian Bold	8.67	0.00	0.00
Irish River	Riverman	12.14	0.00	0.00
Marju	Last Tycoon	9.84	0.00	0.00
Shalford	Thatching	6.30	0.00	0.00
Indian Ridge	Ahonoora	11.34	2.38	0.21
Hadeer	General Assembly	5.29	1.14	0.21
Sayf El Arab	Drone	10.03	2.50	0.25
Manila	Lyphard	14.16	4.55	0.32
Shareef Dancer	Northern Dancer	6.09	1.98	0.33
Warrshan	Northern Dancer	8.70	2.94	0.34
Lugana Beach	Tumble Wind	10.55	3.57	0.34
Imp Society	Barrera	10.99	4.17	0.38
Thatching	Thatch	9.29	3.60	0.39
Fayruz	Song	10.47	4.17	0.40
Batshoof	Sadler's Wells	10.56	4.35	0.41
Rousillon	Riverman	10.73	4.55	0.42
Red Sunset	Red God	10.62	4.84	0.46
Bluebird	Storm Bird	10.53	4.85	0.46
Doulab	Topsider	9.67	4.46	0.46
Cadeaux Genereux	Young Generation	14.44	6.92	0.48

Form Sires

In The Wings	Sadler's Wells	14.36	7.14	0.50
Archway	Thatching	10.94	5.56	0.51
Tragic Role	Nureyev	10.40	5.41	0.52
Bering	Arctic Tern	13.79	7.41	0.54
Komaite	Nureyev	11.50	6.58	0.57
Soviet Star	Nureyev	14.93	9.33	0.63
Never So Bold	Bold Lad (IRE)	6.63	4.30	0.65
Tina's Pet	Mummy's Pet	7.45	4.88	0.65
Mujtahid	Woodman	13.04	8.70	0.67
Don't Forget Me	Ahonoora	8.36	5.61	0.67

Damsire - Rest-Pattern

DAMSIRE	DAMSIRE'S SIRE	OSR	RULE	NEG
Welsh Saint	Sir Paddy	7.89	2.60	0.33
Rainbow Quest	Blushing Groom	14.40	4.76	0.33
Alzao	Lyphard	11.07	4.26	0.38
Hot Spark	Habitat	11.00	4.65	0.42
Irish River	Riverman	13.27	5.68	0.43
Rarity	Hethersett	13.71	6.25	0.46
Pas De Seul	Mill Reef	11.51	5.56	0.48
General Assembly	Secretariat	12.17	6.12	0.50
Hotfoot	Firestreak	11.84	6.00	0.51
Dance In Time	Northern Dancer	10.86	5.75	0.53
Reform	Pall Mall	10.09	5.56	0.55
Great Nephew	Honeyway	8.74	4.84	0.55
Godswalk	Dancer's image	8.45	4.76	0.56
Persian Bold	Bold Lad (IRE)	10.93	6.40	0.59
Secretariat	Bold Ruler	10.96	6.45	0.59
Be My Guest	Northern Dancer	11.16	6.75	0.60
Red Alert	Red God	11.31	7.02	0.62
Majestic Light	Majestic Prince	17.89	11.11	0.62
Caro	Fortino II	12.62	7.89	0.63
Sharpen Up	Atan	10.51	6.77	0.64
Arctic Tern	Sea-Bird II	14.04	9.09	0.65
Troy	Petingo	11.56	8.05	0.70
Miswaki	Mr Prospector	11.90	8.33	0.70

Form Sires

TRACK TYPE

Sire - Track Type (Stiff)

DAMSIRE	SIRE'S SIRE	OSR	RULE	NEG
Mystiko	Secreto	6.97	1.72	0.25
Pursuit Of Love	Groom Dancer	10.97	3.90	0.36
Formidable	Forli	7.48	3.57	0.48
Batshoof	Sadler's Wells	8.70	4.63	0.53
Nordico	Northern Dancer	9.81	5.47	0.56
Manila	Lyphard	16.56	9.38	0.57
Marju	Last Tycoon	11.58	7.07	0.61
Keen	Sharpen Up	7.53	4.67	0.62
Broken Hearted	Dara Monarch	11.63	7.58	0.65
Kalaglow	Kalamoun	13.39	8.76	0.65
Dowsing	Riverman	11.86	8.09	0.68
Shareef Dancer	Northern Dancer	6.17	4.26	0.69
Damister	Mr Prospector	10.09	7.05	0.70
Dashing Blade	Elegant Air	13.10	9.21	0.70

Sire - Track Type (Easy)

DAMSIRE	SIRE'S SIRE	OSR	RULE	NEG
Shalford	Thatching	7.03	1.82	0.26
Silver Hawk	Roberto	13.09	5.66	0.43
Elmaamul	Diesis	12.00	5.63	0.47
Marju	Last Tycoon	11.28	5.66	0.50
Green Dancer	Nijinsky	15.83	8.33	0.53
Doyoun	Mill Reef	16.67	10.00	0.60
Red Ransom	Roberto	18.33	11.11	0.61
Priolo	Sovereign Dancer	11.81	7.32	0.62
Imperial Frontier	Lyphard	6.58	4.17	0.63
Irish River	Riverman	12.78	8.33	0.65
Fairy King	Northern Dancer	13.60	9.36	0.69

Form Sires

Sire - Track Type (Sharp)

DAMSIRE	SIRE'S SIRE	OSR	RULE	NEG
Priolo	Sovereign Dancer	11.81	4.08	0.35
Imperial Frontier	Lyphard	6.58	2.82	0.43
Woodman	Mr Prospector	13.32	6.31	0.47
Damister	Mr Prospector	9.28	4.81	0.52
Pennine Walk	Persian Bold	8.23	4.60	0.56
Ballacashtal	Vice Regent	6.57	3.82	0.58
Salse	Topsider	12.14	7.28	0.60
Salt Dome	Blushing Groom	8.23	5.06	0.62
Shalford	Thatching	7.03	4.35	0.62
Waajib	Try My Best	8.93	5.85	0.66
Mujtahid	Woodman	11.11	7.69	0.69
Forzando	Formidable	8.27	5.73	0.69
Robellino	Roberto	10.09	6.99	0.69
Lahib	Riverman	10.75	7.50	0.70

Sire - Track Type (Galloping)

DAMSIRE	SIRE'S SIRE	OSR	RULE	NEG
Manila	Lyphard	14.71	6.38	0.43
Mystiko	Secreto	4.78	2.27	0.48
Warrshan	Northern Dancer	6.87	3.31	0.48
Sayf El Arab	Drone	11.73	5.83	0.50
Great Commotion	Nureyev	15.89	8.00	0.50
Rousillon	Riverman	13.28	7.01	0.53
Dashing Blade	Elegant Air	13.16	7.02	0.53
Tirol	Thatching	9.12	5.02	0.55
Puissance	Thatching	8.62	5.10	0.59
Dowsing	Riverman	10.99	6.55	0.60
Safawan	Young Generation	9.73	5.94	0.61
Weldnaas	Diesis	5.72	3.55	0.62
Risk Me	Sharpo	6.42	4.33	0.67
Lugana Beach	Tumble Wind	7.63	5.15	0.68
Komaite	Nureyev	8.46	5.84	0.69
Pursuit Of Love	Groom Dancer	9.73	6.72	0.69
Petoski	Niniski	9.14	6.33	0.69
El Gran Senor	Northern Dancer	16.19	11.24	0.69
Batshoof	Sadler's Wells	7.86	5.48	0.70
Superlative	Nebbiolo	8.42	5.88	0.70
Rainbow Quest	Blushing Groom	14.36	10.11	0.70

Form Sires

Sire - Track Type (Undulating)

DAMSIRE	SIRE'S SIRE	OSR	RULE	NEG
Mystiko	Secreto	4.78	0.00	0.00
Tragic Role	Nureyev	14.13	7.04	0.50
Priolo	Sovereign Dancer	11.81	6.00	0.51
Dominion	Derring-Do	9.97	5.15	0.52
Elmaamul	Diesis	12.00	6.85	0.57
Lahib	Riverman	10.75	6.25	0.58
Marju	Last Tycoon	11.28	6.76	0.60
Polish Precedent	Danzig	13.50	8.26	0.61
Robellino	Roberto	10.09	6.21	0.62
Interrex	Vice Regent	8.00	5.10	0.64
Damister	Mr Prospector	9.28	6.06	0.65
Petoski	Niniski	9.14	6.00	0.66
Irish River	Riverman	12.78	8.51	0.67
Batshoof	Sadler's Wells	7.86	5.33	0.68

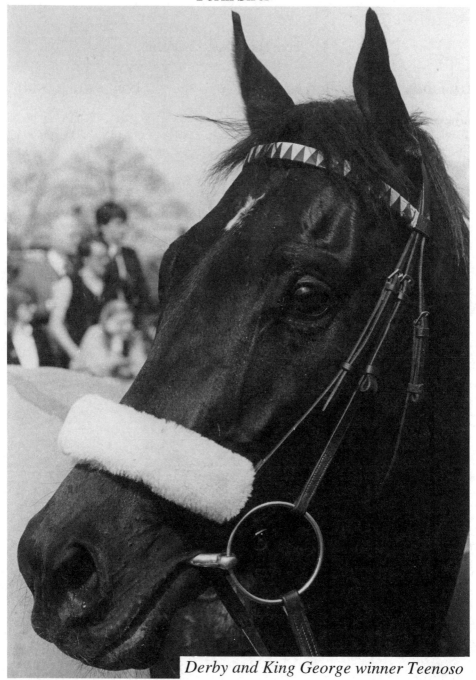

Derby and King George winner Teenoso

Form Sires

Chapter 14

Dosage Theory Explained

The popularity of dosage theory is on the increase in the UK, and I am aware that a book of this nature should be giving it a good airing. Thankfully, I have been able to enlist the services of someone who is able cover the subject in much greater detail than I ever could. Kathleen Jones is a Pedigree Researcher in Lexington, Kentucky.

DOSAGE THEORY by Kathleen Jones

Dosage is a mathematical analysis of the strengths in a thoroughbred pedigree based upon the location of certain outstanding sires in its family. While never designed to be a handicapping tool, that is its most popular use today.

A horse's dosage figures express a good deal about the animal, and what the animal was bred for, in numerical terms. The first thing to understand is where the numbers come from. And the answer is - pedigree. Specifically, it is the influential sires in the pedigree which contribute the points to the dosage analysis.

About 200 stallions at this time have been recognized as Chefs-de-Race (Masters of the Breed). In general, they are the stallions which have had a remarkable influence on the breed over the last century; the names which remain like Nearco, Round Table, Bold Ruler, etc. when other stallions of short-lived popularity have disappeared.

Depending on the generation in which it appears, the stallion contributes a certain number of points to the subject horse. Round Table in the 2nd generation, for instance, contributes more points than Round Table in the 3rd generation. This follows the assumption that the influence becomes less and less evident with each passing generation. A first generation sire contributes 16 points (if he's listed on the Chef-de-Race list); a second generation sire contributes 8 points; 3rd generation contributes 4 points; and 4th generation 2 points.

Chef-de-Race stallions have been assigned to one or more of these categories: Brilliant - Intermediate - Classic - Solid - Professional. These five categories represent the spectrum of speed (Brilliant) to stamina (Professional). Just as a prism separates light into definite visible bands, dosage separates a horse's inherited aptitudes into definite visible categories.

A Brilliant chef is one who has been identified as one who tends to produce runners who excel at extremely short distances. His appearance in the pedigree will improve the runner's Brilliant score. Conversely, a Professional chef tends to

Form Sires

produce runners who excel at extremely long distances. Classic chefs tend to produce good "Classic" distance runners and so on.

Some stallions have been named a Chef in more than one category, like Mr Prospector who is a "Brilliant/Classic" Chef. If he appears in the foal's pedigree, his allowable points will be split between those two categories. For instance, if he appears in the 2nd generation in the pedigree, he is worth 8 points to the foal. Four points are added to the Brilliant score, and four points are added to the Classic score.

The first expression of dosage figures is the "profile". This is a series of five numbers which show the reader exactly how many points this horse has inherited from sires in each category. Look at these examples:

DEMALOOT DEMASHOOT	profile=15-10-7-0-0	DI=8.14	CD= 1.25
SPRING MARATHON	profile= 7-2-9-5-11	DI= 0.66	CD= -0.32

For Demaloot Demashoot, notice how the largest number (15) appears in the Brilliant category. Note also how the entire profile slants toward the speed end of the spectrum. This is the profile of a sprinter. The horse's race record bears that out. All of his victories came at 6 furlongs or less, including triumphs in the Clarinet King Stakes and the Count Fleet Sprint [Grade 3] in which he scorched the six panels in 1:08 1/5!

Now compare the profile of Spring Marathon. It's quite different. This profile slants to the right, indicating a propensity for stamina. Note how the largest of the figures appears in the Professional category Once again, his race record concurs. On the Flat he placed at 11 1/2 furlongs and 14 furlongs, then graduated to even longer tests. Over jumps, he has been successful even beyond 3 miles. The dosage profile clearly points to distance capabilities for this horse.

The dosage index (DI) is simply the ratio of speed points to stamina points. Everything to the left of middle is speed. Everything to the right of middle is stamina. The Classic category (in the middle) is divided equally between speed and stamina.

For Demaloot Demashoot, 15 + 10 + 3 1/2 are his speed points. That makes 28 1/2 speed points. On the right side we have 3 1/2 + 0 + 0, for a total of 3 1/2 stamina points. Divide speed by stamina. 28 1/2 divided by 3 1/2 equals 8.14. This means the horse has over 8 times as much speed as stamina.

For Spring Marathon, the index is 0.66, indicating that he has only two-thirds as much speed as stamina. Just for your information - more stamina than speed often flags a good turf performer.

Form Sires

The most famous use of dosage is in handicapping the Kentucky Derby. You may have heard that any horse with a DI greater than 4.00 cannot win the Derby. This figure was selected not by people, but by history because no horse with a higher DI has ever won the race. (Strike the Gold won with a DI of 9.0 only because Alydar was yet to be named to the Chef-de-Race list in the Classic category. After that designation, the DI for Strike the Gold fell to the more realistic figure of 2.6.). The 4.0 barrier is a good historical yardstick but is bound to be broken someday - simply because horses do not race against distances, they race against other horses.

The Center of Distribution (CD) marks the balancing point of all the numbers in the profile. Picture a see-saw with weights of various sizes randomly distributed along its length. Where does the fulcrum need to be placed to balance the see-saw? That's what the CD is. It comes from a slightly more complex formula. If you are interested, the formula is: [(Bril x 2) + Int] - [Solid + (Prof x 2)] / total points

The result of this formula will always be a number between +2 and -2. If you were to assign the value +2 to the Brilliant category, +1 to Intermediate, and so on as shown here, you will have created a gauge for viewing the Center of Distribution.

Brilliant	Intermediate	Classic	Solid	Professional
+2	+1	0	-1	-2

For Demaloot Demashoot, the CD is 1.25. This means the imaginary fulcrum must be moved to the left, all the way to the +1.25 mark on this scale. That marks the perfect balancing point for Demaloot Demashoot's unique dosage profile. For Spring Marathon, whose CD is -0.32, the fulcrum must be moved to the right, into the negative numbers, into the realm of stayers.

All thoroughbreds are bred for a specific distance. The CD points to that approximate distance. Below is a scale, which although not absolute, may show how the Center of Distribution can help indicate the ideal distance for the horse:

Furlongs = 4 5 6 7 8 9 10 11 12 13 14 15 16 17 18+

CD Scale = +2 . . . . +1 . . . . 0 . . . . -1 . . . . -2

Brilliant   Inter   Classic   Solid   Professional

Sprint champion LOCHSONG was phenomenally fast, and posted most of her victories at the five- furlong distance. Her profile shows why.

LOCHSONG   profile = 6-0-0-0-0   DI= Infinity   CD= 2.00

Form Sires

When the word "infinity" is used for a Dosage Index, it simply means that there are no stamina points present with which to make the calculation. A whole number cannot be divided by zero. Some people prefer to show this as the numerical result of "0". Either way it is a clear flag that the runner has no stamina. It is also possible, although rare, to see a profile with stamina points only, and no speed, such as in a profile like this: 0-0-0-2-10. This would also result in an Infinity index.

If a two-mile race were written for the entrants Lochsong, Demaloot Demashoot, and Spring Marathon, which would be the most likely choice to win? Which has the best inherited advantages? Which has the lowest CD? That's the benefit in knowing the Center of Distribution.

HANDICAPPING WITH DOSAGE

Here's an example of how the first race at Churchill Downs on June 25, 1997 may have been handicapped using this method. This was a 5 1/2 furlong race for 2yo fillies, and most of the field were previously unraced. The entrants in alphabetical order were:

HORSE	PROFILE	DI	CD
Culpepper Cady	5-1-3-0-1	3.00	0.90
Dertie Bertie	2-0-7-0-1	1.22	0.20
Dontcatchme Please	5-1-10-2-0	1.57	0.50
Fleet Lady Hawk	10-5-9-0-0	4.33	1.04
Goldy's Prize	3-0-7-0-0	1.86	0.60
Heartache Dyna	7-2-21-1-1	1.56	0.41
Her Own Agenda	10-7-7-2-0	3.73	0.96
Oye Commo Va	13-4-3-0-0	12.33	1.50
Reggie Lane	5-2-10-2-1	1.50	0.40
Smokem N Smile	11-5-10-0-0	4.20	1.04
Tway	3-1-7-3-0	1.15	0.29

A 5 1/2 furlong sprint should require some Brilliant speed. The one entrant which has the greatest Brilliant score is Oye Como Va. One should also look for high DI and high CD figures for sprints. Again - Oye Como Va ranks the highest. She would have been the most likely pick using dosage as the sole criteria.

The result of the race was that Oye Como Va won, paying $121.60 on a $2 win ticket.

Form Sires

Another example. The 2:20 at Huntingdon on October 21, 1997. This was a threemile & two-furlong hurdle, so stamina would be a benefit. The field in alphabetical order:

HORSE	PROFILE	DI	CD
Brindley House	7-0-7-4-8	0.68	0.23
Marsh's Law	3-1-4-0-0	3.00	0.88
Polo Pony	2-0-2-2-0	1.00	0.33
San Giorgio	2-2-13-0-3	1.11	0.00
Snow Board	10-2-9-4-3	1.43	0.43
Spring Marathon	7-2-9-5-11	0.66	0.32
Tharsis	10-2-6-2-2	2.14	0.73

The one entrant here which possesses the greatest stock of stamina is Spring Marathon. Brindley House is also quite good, and San Giorgio also earns a rather low CD based upon the lack of any serious speed points. The lowest DI score also goes to Spring Marathon. He would be the logical pick in this event if using dosage as the sole criteria.

The result was that despite being highweighted at 12 stone, Spring Marathon won at odds of 6-to-1 by eventually overcoming San Giorgio at the finish.

BREEDING WITH DOSAGE

The most popular use of dosage among breeders is in determining a good stallion match for a particular mare. After all other considerations have been made, such as location, stud fee, desired crosses, etc., dosage can be employed to narrow the possibilities further. As an example, let us assume that you own the American champion juvenile filly Countess Diana and the time has come to breed her. For fun - let us say that stud fee is no object, so you have narrowed your target stallions down to these five Kentucky standouts: Seattle Slew, Glitterman, Unbridled, Go For Gin, and Gone West.

By calculating the dosage figures of the hypothetical offspring, one can "preview" the result. Here are the figures for each hypothetical mating:

DAM+SIRE	PROFILE	DI	CD
Countess Diana + Seattle Slew	10-5-15-2-0	2.37	0.72
Countess Diana + Glitterman	8-7-7-0-0	5.29	1.05
Countess Diana + Unbridled	6-4-8-0-6	1.40	0.17
Countess Diana + Go For Gin	4-5-12-2-3	1.36	0.19
Countess Diana + Gone West	10-9-13-0-0	3.92	0.91

Form Sires

Remember that these figures are for the resulting offspring, not for the stallions themselves. At this point, the breeder should already know what the goal of the mating is to be. Is a sprinter desired? Is a classic-distance runner desired? Perhaps a decent turf miler?

If the goal is to breed a sprinter, then Glitterman should be considered. The profile of his foal is definitely speed-biased, and the DI and CD figures are the highest of these options.

If a distance runner is the goal, then Unbridled and Go For Gin should be considered since the resulting DI and CD are both quite low. Both also possess far more Solid and/or Professional points than the average American runner, and therefore have the potential of being superior runners over a distance of ground.

Seattle Slew and Gone West result in similar profiles, both with large Brilliant and Classic scores. A large Brilliant score is very commercial. Juvenile runners tend not to be physically mature enough to tackle the long distances they have been bred for. They tend to tap into the Brilliant and Intermediate wells first, then later mature into the stamina wing of the profile. Since American two-year-olds are never asked to run a distance anyway, the large Brilliant figure may indicate those which can excel in the juvenile year.

The large Classic score of these two stallions indicates that the potential for "maturing into distance" is present. Buyers are sure to be especially attracted to well-conformed and attractive foals which have been bred for this type of versatility. You can see how dosage would be a helpful tool in planning a breeding.

KATHLEEN M. JONES is a pedigree researcher in Lexington, Kentucky, whose special field of interest is International Racing. Her interest in dosage analysis began after reading a magazine article written by Dr. Stephen Roman, the inventor of the "Dosage Index". Since that time, she has found dosage to be a useful additional tool to other handicapping methods. She attributes her successful selection of Arcangues in the 1993 Breeders' Cup Classic (at odds of 133-to-1) to a basic understanding of dosage theory.

Chefs de Race

Dr Stephen Roman's list of Chefs de Race

See his Web site at: http://www.chefs-de-race.com/

Abernant (B)
Ack Ack (I/C)
Admiral Drake (P)
Alcantara II (P)
Alibhai (C)
Alizier (P)
Alycidon (P)
Alydar (C)
Apalachee (B)
Asterus (S)
Aureole (C)
Bachelor's Double (S)
Bahram (C)
Baldski (B/I)
Ballymoss (S)
Bayardo (P)
Ben Brush (I)
Best Turn (C)
Big Game (I)
Black Toney (B/I)
Blandford (C)
Blenheim II (C/S)
Black Larkspur (C)
Blushing Groom (B/C)
Bois Roussel (S)
Bold Bidder (I/C)
Bold Ruler (B/I)
Brantome (C)
British Empire (B)
Broomstick (I)
Bruleur (P)
Buckpasser (C)
Bull Dog (B)
Bull Lea (C)
Caro (I/C)
Chateau Bouscaut (P)
Chaucer (S)
Cicero (I)
Clarissimus (C)
Colorado (I)
Congreve (I)
Count Fleet (C)
Court Martial (B)
Creme dela Creme (C/S)
Crepello (P)
Damascus (I/C)
Danzig (I/C)
Dark Ronald (P)

Discovery (S)
Djebel (I)
Donatello II (P)
Double Jay (B)
Eight Thirty (I)
Equipoise (I/C)
Exclusive Native (C)
Fair Play (S/P)
Fair Trial (B)
Fairway (B)
Forli (C)
Foxbridge (P)
Full Sail (I)
Gainsborough (C)
Gallant Man (B/I)
Graustark (C/S)
Grey Dawn II (B/I)
Grey Soverign (B)
Gundomar (C)
Habitat (B)
Hail To Reason (C)
Halo (B/C)
Havresac II (I)
Heliopolis (B)
Herbager (C/S)
High Top (C)
His Majesty (C)
Hoist The Flag (B/I)
Hurry On (P)
Hyperion (B/C)
Icecapade (B/C)
In Reality (B/C)
Intentionally (B/I)
Key To The Mint (B/C)
Khaled (I)
King Salmon (I)
King's Bishop (B/I)
La Farina (P)
Le Fabuleux (P)
Luthier (C)
Lyphard (C)
Mahmoud (I/C)
Man O' War (I/C)
Massine (P)
Midstream (C)
Mieuxce (P)
Mill Reef (C/S)
Mossborough (C)

Mr Prospector (B/C)
My Babu (B)
Nashua (I/C)
Nasrullah (B)
Native Dancer (I/C)
Navarro (C)
Nearco (B/C)
Never Bend (B/I)
Never Say Die (C)
Nijinsky II (C/S)
Noholme II (B/C)
Northern Dancer (B/C)
Nureyev (C)
Oleander (S)
Olympia (B)
Orby (B)
Ortello (P)
Panorama (B)
Persian Gulf (C)
Peter Pan (B)
Petition (I)
Phalaris (B)
Pharis II (B)
Pharos (I)
Pia Star (S)
Pilate (C)
Polynesian (I)
Pompey (B)
Precipitation (P)
Pretense (C)
Prince Bio (C)
Prince Chevalier (C)
Prince john (C)
Princequillo (I/S)
Prince Rose (C)
Promised Land (C)
Rabelais (P)
Raise A Native (B)
Relko (S)
Reviewer (B/C)
Ribot (C/P)
Right Royal (S)
Riverman (I/C)
Roberto (C)
Rock Sand (C/S)
Roman (B/I)
Round Table (S)

Royal Charger (B)
Run The Gantlet (P)
Sardanapale (P)
Sea-Bird (S)
Seattle Slew (B/C)
Secretariat (I/C)
Sharpen Up (B/C)
Sicambre (C)
Sideral (C)
Sir Cosmo (B)
Sir Gallahad III (C)
Sir Gaylord (I/C)
Sir Ivor (I/C)
Solario (P)
Son-In-Law (P)
Speak John (B/I)
Spearmint (P)
py Song (B)
Stage Door Johnny (S/P)
Star Kingdom (I/C)
Star Shoot (I)
Sunny Boy (P)
Sunstar (S)
Sweep (I)
Swynford (C)
T V Lark (I)
Tantieme (S)
Teddy (S)
The Tetrarch (I)
Ticino (C/S)
Tom Fool (I/C)
Tom Rolfe (C/P)
Tourbillon (C/P)
Tracery (C)
Traghetto (I)
Tudor Minstrel (B)
Turn-To (B/I)
Ultimus (B)
Vaguely Noble (C/P)
Vandale (P)
Vatellor (P)
Vatout (S)
Vieux Manoir (C)
War Admiral (C)
What A Pl'sure (B)
Wild Risk (P)
Worden (S)

109

Zafonic produced a very classy first crop of juveniles in 1997

Form Sires

Chapter 15

First Season Sires (1997)

First-season sires of 1997 have not been included in the performance tables because their progeny have not raced enough for sufficient data to have accumulated. However, this will not prevent us from examining their progeny's record to date, and also looking at the pedigree of each sire to see what traits may reveal themselves in their progeny as they begin to race as three-year-olds.

The comments which follow the data will hopefully show the versatility of pedigree handicapping, and encourage you to come up with some ideas of your own.

ZAFONIC   Gone West - Zaizafon (The Minstrel)
Dosage Profile: 11-5-10-0-0   DI: 4.20   CD: 1.04
Progeny Record:
W-R: 13-34 (38%),   WNRS-RNRS: 9-15 (60%),   WIN MONEY: £237,000
GOING: SFT 0-3, GS 1-2 (50%), GD 8-16 (50%), GF 4-13 (30%)
DISTANCE: 5F 2-3 (66%), 6F 4-12 (33%), 7F 7-17 (41%), 8F 0-2

Zafonic produced a very classy crop of two-year-olds in his first season. They managed to win between them two Group One races, a Group Three race and a listed event, as well as six placed efforts in Group company. When his son, Xaar, won the Dewhurst at Newmarket in October (beating the useful Tamarisk by seven lengths) it put beyond doubt the fact that here was a sire of immense potential.

Zafonic's OSR of 38% makes very good reading, but my one concern is that his stock may not make the improvement generally expected of horses from 2 to 3 years. His sire, Gone West, has a very respectable strike rate of 25% with his 2yo progeny, but this falls sharply to 12% when they race as three-year-olds. This precocity within his stock may also explain why Zafonic has made such a good start in his first season, and that hot two-year-olds such as Xaar may not have much improvement in them. I am sure they will perform very well in the first half of 1998, but, like Zafonic himself (who did little else after winning the Guineas) where will they go from that point on?

One way of testing to see which of Zafonic's progeny will beat the precocity trap is to look at the damsire of each offspring. Hopefully they will possess enough 'late-maturity' genes for there to be some sort of balance between early brilliance and future potential. Xaar is represented by Sir Ivor, then we have three unbeaten horses by the same sire (with their damsires in brackets), Fantasy Island (Mill Reef), Zaya (Secreto) and Pontoon (Riverman).

Form Sires

Damsires

Sir Ivor:	2 y-o: 9-131 (7%)	3 y-o: 40-337 (12%)
Mill Reef:	2 y-o: 33-217 (15%)	3 y-o: 95-506 (19%)
Secreto:	2 y-o: 11-57 (19%)	3 y-o: 14-91 (15%)
Riverman:	2 y-o: 23-161 (14%)	3 y-o: 42-275 (15%)

There is hope for Xaar yet! These figures clearly show that progeny with Sir Ivor as their damsire progress most from 2 to 3 years. This means that Xaar has a good chance of achieving continuing success during his three-year-old career.

Looking to Gone West for other pointers, it is clear by his record that his progeny much prefer firm ground (19%) to soft (7%), and, as can be seen above, Zafonic's progeny have failed on their three attempts to win on the soft. So, if conditions are testing underfoot at Newmarket in May there could still be a major upset.

TENBY   Caerleon - Shining Water (Kalaglow)
Dosage Profile: 3-2-10-11-0   DI: 0.62   CD: -0.12
Progeny Record:
W-R: 9-56 (16%),   WNRS-RNRS: 5-16 (31%),   WIN MONEY: £52,000
GOING: HVY 1-3 (33%),   SFT 1-5 (20%),   GS 2-15 (13%),   GD 2-19 (10%), GF 3-14 (30%)
DISTANCE: 5F 1-3 (33%),   6F 3-15 (20%),   7F 2-24 (8%),   8F 2-12 (16%), 9F 1-2 (50%)

Both Caerleon (sire) and Kalaglow (damsire) strongly favour firm ground, so it was a little surprising to see a combined total of 4 wins from 23 runs (17%) from the progeny of Tenby on going slower than good. However, two of these victories came at eight and nine furlongs respectively, and I would say it was more the influence for stamina which came into play on both occasions. When the progeny of Tenby encountered ground firmer than good they achieved a strike rate of 30%, and I would predict that they, and other offspring, will be even more at home on ground that is firmer still.

As well as a liking for firm ground, and an ability to stay, Caerleon and Kalaglow also produce stock which improves its strike rate from two to three years of age. So look out for those improving three-year-olds by Tenby who are stepping up in distance, they should more than pay their way - especially if the track is riding fast.

Carry The Flag, a son of Tenby who won two of his four starts as a two-year-old, won his final race of the season over eight furlongs at Warwick. *Raceform* Note

Form Sires

Book comments summed things up nicely when they wrote: "Carry The Flag, a half-brother to Posidonas, showed just how well he stays on this faster ground."

GREENSMITH   Known Fact - Infra Green (Laser Light)
Dosage Profile: 9-3-10-0-2   DI: 2.43   CD: 0.71
Progeny Record:
W-R: 14-35 (40%),   WNRS-RNRS: 4-6 (66%),   WIN MONEY: £43,000
GOING: HVY 1-1 (100%), SFT 2-4 (50%), GD 4-8 (50%), GF 5-10 (50%),
FM 1-6 (16%)
DISTANCE: 5F 6-19 (31%), 6F 2-6 (33%), 7F 6-9 (66%), 8F 0-1

Greensmith's attractive OSR of 40% is due mainly to the exploits of two multi-winning two-year-olds, namely, Lord Smith (six wins) and Prince Foley (five wins). This 'winability' can be traced back to Greensmith's paternal grandsire, In Reality, who won fourteen races between the ages of two and four.

Greensmith was a sharp two-year-old, winning three of his four starts, all at seven furlongs. He then won a couple of handicaps in May of the following year (at seven and eight furlongs) before running third behind Shining Steel in the Diomed Stakes (Group 3) at Epsom, and then second to Shaadi in the St James's Palace Stakes (Group 1) at Royal Ascot.

Because of the precocity within his stock I would say his progeny are likely to follow in his footsteps and be effective early in the season of their third year, winning at distances of seven and eight furlongs, and on all types of going.

BRIEF TRUCE   Irish River - Falafel (Northern Dancer)
Dosage Profile: 9-9-12-0-2   DI: 3.00   CD: 0.72
Progeny Record:
W-R: 12-132 (9%),   WNRS-RNRS: 9-34 (26%),   WIN MONEY: £62,000
GOING: HVY 0-3, SFT 1-19 (5%), GS 7-37 (18%), GD 2-30 (6%), GF 0-35,
FM 1-5 (20%)
DISTANCE: 5F 7-32 (21%), 6F 4-40 (5%), 7F 1-35 (2%), 8F 2-22 (9%), 9F
0-2

Brief Truce did not see a racecourse until his third year, but he quickly made up for lost time by winning four of his ten races. His crowning moment came at Royal Ascot when he won the St James's Palace Stakes (Group 1) over a mile.

If we assume that he needed time to develop sufficiently before starting his racing career, then we may be surprised to find that the progeny of his sire, Irish River, achieve a higher strike rate at two than they do at three. However, the stock of his paternal grandsire, Riverman, improve from two to three, so which are we to trust as the more likely to pass on their influence?

When things are not so clear cut it often pays to look to the female side of the pedigree, and here we find Northern Dancer (the maternal grandsire of Brief Truce). Northern Dancer's progeny achieve a strike rate of 15% as two-year-olds, and a strike rate of over 20% when they run at three. This gives more weight to the idea that the progeny of Brief Truce will need a little time before showing their true potential.

Looking at the improvement tables for sires whose progeny can carry weight, we see that Irish River (0.44), Riverman (0.62) and Northern Dancer (0.63) all score very poor results, so it would seem necessary to avoid the progeny of Brief Truce if they are asked to shoulder weight.

That said, I like the look of the pedigree of Brief Truce. His stock already have a touch of class about them (four placed efforts in Group company), and should be noted when racing at distances between eight and ten furlongs, especially if the ground comes up soft, because both Riverman (1.33) and Northern Dancer (1.28) score well.

HAMAS   Danzig - Fall Aspen (Pretense)
Dosage Profile: 8-13-25-0-0   DI: 2.68   CD: 0.63
Progeny Record:
W-R: 9-44 (20%), WNRS-RNRS: 4-11 (36%), WIN MONEY: £48,000
GOING: HVY 0-1, SFT 0-5, GS 4-6 (66%), GD 2-14 (14%), GF 3-15 (20%), FM 0-2
DISTANCE: 5F 0-10. 6F 7-21 (33%), 7F 1-11 (9%), 8F 1-2 (50%)

The two-year-old progeny of Hamas scored nine wins from forty-four starts to record an OSR of 20%. Five of these victories were earned by the same horse - Regal Revolution - and all over a trip of six furlongs. No other two-year-old from the same crop even came close to winning as many races, so what was it that made this horse so special?

Well, Regal Revolution's paternal grandsire, Danzig, has an improvement rating of 1.38 for his two-year-old progeny, which means he is more than capable of getting early sorts, while on the female side of his pedigree we find the damsire Silver Hawk, who also scores well in this department (on the sires listing), showing a rating of 1.33. It is more than likely that Regal Revolution has benefited from having two sires within his immediate pedigree whose offspring show such precocity.

Encouragingly, both Danzig (17%) and Silver Hawk (16%) still achieve a very respectable strike rate with their three-year-old progeny, and they are usually of a high quality (eleven Group winners between them in the last four years). The progeny of both sires are well at home on firm ground, though some Danzigs do not mind it on the soft side of good. Silver Hawk's progeny score very poorly when asked to carry weight (0.14), with Danzig's offspring not doing much to redress the balance at 0.90.

If we take Regal Revolution out of the equation the strike rate for Hamas's two-year-old runners takes a dive. However, worry not, because his dosage profile strongly suggests his progeny will do better over distances of between ten and twelve furlongs - which is the domain of horses aged three years and above.

> **LION CAVERN**   Mr Prospector - Secrettame (Secretariat)
> **Dosage Profile**: 24-14-19-1-0   DI: 4.52   CD: 1.05
> **Progeny Record**:
> W-R: 10-69 (14%),   WNRS-RNRS: 7-24 (29%),   WIN MONEY: £53,000
> GOING: HVY 0-2,   SFT 0-5,   GS 0-5,   GD 4-24 (16%),   GF 3-29 (10%),
> FM 2-2 (100%)
> DISTANCE: 5F 0-2,   6F 2-26 (7%),   7F 6-36 (16%),   8F 2-5 (40%)

The first thing to note about Lion Cavern is that he is a full-brother to Gone West, so we should expect his two-year-old stock to be well forward. However, he only manages an OSR of 14% with his two-year-old runners, with most of them winning at seven and eight furlongs. His sire, Mr Prospector, and damsire, Secretariat, are also influences for early maturity, so it seems surprising that his stock have under-achieved so far.

It is no surprise to see that his progeny have won two out of two on firm ground, as this seems to be a strong trait within the family, but three wins from twenty-nine runs on good-to-firm going is still rather disappointing.

The progeny of Lion Cavern improve their strike rate the further they travel, which I would attribute to the influence of his damsire, Secretariat, who, on the improvement table for two-year-olds over a mile, scored very highly. Mr Prospector, his sire, is more an influence for juvenile speed, but with the progeny of Lion Cavern only scoring two wins from twenty-eight starts at five and six furlongs, we can start to believe that he does not take after his father in this department.

Lion Cavern may be a full-brother to Gone West, but I think here the similarity may end. It could be that Gone West takes more after his sire, Mr Prospector (with the performance tables supporting this view), while Lion Cavern could very much be tracing the footsteps of his maternal grandsire, Secretariat, in that his stock will get further and develop more as three-year-olds.

Form Sires

PETARDIA   Petong - What A Pet (Mummy's Pet)
Dosage Profile: 8-1-1-2-0   DI: 3.80   CD: 1.25
Progeny Record:
W-R: 13-214 (6%),   WNRS-RNRS: 8-40 (20%),   WIN MONEY: £90,000
GOING: HVY 1-3 (33%), SFT 1-17 (5%), GS 2-31 (6%), GD 4-70 (5%), GF 5-75 (6%), FM 0-8
DISTANCE: 5F 4-63 (6%), 6F 4-59 (6%), 7F 4-74 (5%), 8F 1-17 (5%)

Petardia may not have the most fashionable of pedigrees, but there is still a lot to get excited about when looking at his ancestry.

His sire, Petong, had a highly successful three-year-old career, winning six of his nine races. He then improved further as a four-year-old to win the Wokingham (carrying 9-6), Stewards' Cup (9-10), and finally the Group Two Vernons Sprint Cup at Haydock.

Petong's weight-carrying performances in those two big handicaps show that he has ability in the weight-carrying department, and a look at the record of his progeny shows that the trait is being handed down. Petong's OSR is 7%, which rises to 11% when his progeny are asked to carry weight, and then rises again to a staggering 33% when we restrict those qualifiers to a distance of five furlongs.

Interestingly, there is a weight-carrying influence on the female side of Petardia's pedigree too. His damsire, Mummy's Pet, features three times on the sires improvement table for weight, being responsible for three of the listed sires. And Mummy's Pet sire, Sing Sing, has already shown himself to be an influence for weight earlier in this book. So, all in all, we have in Petardia a sire who may not get Classic winners, but his progeny sure as hell should be able to shoulder weight!

My next task was to log on to the Website of the British Racing Centre. All progeny of Petardia should be followed when carrying weight, but I wanted to find out which ones had an influence for weight on the female side of their pedigrees (which would make them even more backable). I asked the computer to list all progeny in training by the sire Petardia, and within seconds the information was on my screen. I looked at the damsire of each runner to see if a weight influence was present.

Name Of Love, winner of three of her four races as a two-year-old, is out of a mare by Shareef Dancer, who scores a very impressive 2.01 on the sire improvement table for weight.

Jimmy Swift, unplaced in his only start as a juvenile, is out of a mare by Alzao, who features on the sires consistency table for weight.

Form Sires

Sweet Rosie, best effort when second in a Lingfield maiden, is out of a mare by Mummy's Pet, which means she is inbred to Mummy's Pet (3x2). When a sire is said to be inbred it means it features more than once in the pedigree of a horse (usually within the first four generations). 3x2 means that Mummy's Pet is found in the third generation on the male side of the pedigree, and in the second generation on the female side.

Perhaps as a sign of things to come, the only two-year-old by Petardia to carry 9-7 or over in a handicap during last season was Halmahera, who trotted up over six furlongs at odds of 11-4.

Clantime has a speed profile and a maximum Centre of Distribution

Form Sires

Chapter 16

The Future Of Pedigree Handicapping

This book is probably the first of its kind to be published in the UK. However, I predict that it will soon be superseded by paper publications and software that will give much more sire and damsire information. The details within these mighty tomes (also available on disk) will have been generated by computer programs designed to squeeze the last drop of pedigree information from the form book. I cannot wait for it to happen.

What pedigree handicapping needs is an information explosion, the force of which reaches beyond those fortunate enough to be wired up to the Internet. I was recently told that I should not hope for such advances as this might weaken my position as 'pedigree information provider' but I think this is missing the point.

If people are to develop an interest in pedigree handicapping then what they need is exposure to it, not to be fed information on a need-to-know basis. I am sure many people would like to respond to the articles I write in my Form Sires column for *Raceform Update*, but are unable to do so because they lack the facility to investigate any of the points I make. All of this could be about to change.

Computers are coming down in price all the time, and today you can get a lot of machine for a little money. They give you all the memory capacity you will ever need, and they are also capable of churning through data at a tremendous speed. Research on a single sire that used to take hours, days or weeks, can now be done in a matter of minutes (if not seconds). The software is not standing still either. *Raceform* have told me that they hope to include a damsire search facility on release of Version 4 of *Computer Raceform*, with the mouth-watering prospect that they might also add a 'list-sires' button to their front end. This would enable the user to enter a simple query (such as a weight rule), press the 'list-sires' button, and have on screen a full listing of sires (with their relevant weight-carrying information) within a matter of minutes. This 'killer application' could open up pedigree handicapping to a whole new audience, as, until now, the prospect of working through a list of a couple of hundred sires has been rather an arduous task - even with a lightning-fast computer.

Maybe then the mail I receive in response to my column will start to grow, as more and more people begin to conduct their own pedigree research and generate their own sire tables. Many more theories could be put forward and tested, advancing our understanding of racehorses and what makes them tick.

Beware, once you get bitten by the PH bug you will want to know more, and that is when, if you're not going to die of frustration, you will link up to the Internet.

Form Sires

Pedigree Handicappers live on a diet of racing facts and figures, and on the Internet you will find every kind of resource available. I have recently subscribed to the British Racing Centre, whose very helpful advisor, Jenny Root, got me connected to their Website within a matter of minutes. Here you will find most of what you require to apply PH to events which are happening now. Not least because the site offers you the facility to download a three-generation pedigree for any horse in training. This, as far as I am aware, has never been possible before, which probably goes a long way to explaining why PH has been slow to take off. The site also lets you do a progeny search, which means you can enter the name of a sire and it will come back with the names of all progeny who are currently in training (along with the names of their dam and damsire). Very useful. Throw in a full racecard and results service and the BRC has things pretty well sewn up.

Albin Warth's Thoroughbred Pedigree Query is also a 'must visit' for anyone who is interested in racing. Here you can download a four generation pedigree of most sires and damsires, along with their dosage profiles, dosage index and centre of distribution figures. The dosage figures are based on Steve Roman's list of Chefs-de-Race and, as Steve was the creator of the dosage index, they carry most credibility.

Moving away from the Internet, I also think that pedigree handicapping will play an increasingly important role in how trainers place their horses. Once pedigree information is out there, and has proven to be reliable, then it won't be long before some trainers will be looking at the data to see where the best opportunities lie. If I were a trainer, and I had a horse by a rest-pattern sire, then I would be planning my touch to coincide with the horse returning to the track after a lay-off. If the sire was also an influence for weight-carrying ability, I would also make sure that he was carrying ten stone in a handicap against lowly opposition! Seriously, it will not be long before trainers are using Pedigree Handicappers in much the same way as some use form and speed analysts today.

Also, I am sure breeders and bloodstock agents could benefit greatly from a knowledge of pedigree handicapping. After all, the data it generates is directly related to the racecourse performance of a sire's progeny, and if, for example, the progeny of a sire shows that it cannot handle stiff tracks, then maybe this weakness should be exposed. Not what the marketing people would want I am sure, but at least PH would offer some sort of balance in a world that is populated mainly by 'good news'.

I have been told by some racing information providers that more and more people are considering pedigree when analysing form. Though maybe a little too soon to call it a groundswell of interest in pedigree handicapping, I am sure it will not be long before it receives more column inches in the racing press. In America, the Daily Racing Form already includes sire information within its pages, so it should not be too long before it happens here.

Form Sires

Dick Whitford, legendary form expert for the Sporting Life a few decades ago, once wrote that he hoped to see the day when the Form Book and the Stud Book would come together and answer some of the great handicapping mysteries. He admitted that he had not been able to make the vital links that would have given him so many of the answers, but believed that it was only a matter of time before it did happen. Dick Whitford did not have the benefit of the information technology that is available today, and was quoted as saying that his job, at times, was 'a bloody hard grind'. Had he had this new technology I am sure that he, and the likes of Phil Bull, would have been pedigree handicapping their way to even more success.

This book is just a small step along the road to a greater understanding of what makes racehorses tick. I hope it encourages you to conduct your own research and construct your own sire tables. I would like nothing more than for my mailbag to be bursting with information and ideas from those who had chosen to study pedigree handicapping. Then I would know that it had finally made it into the consciousness of the majority of horseplayers. It may not provide all the answers, but it has the capability of uncovering some of the great handicapping mysteries.

Rock City has a miler's profile with the accent on speed

Form Sires

Chapter 17

Pedigree Information Resources

Computer Raceform (Weekly)
Official Form Book on a disk. Complete with Systems Analyser which enables the user to interrogate the database for racehorse and sire information. Will soon have the capability to analyse damsire data.

> Raceform Ltd, Compton, Newbury, Berkshire, RG20 6NL.
> Tel: 01635 578080.
> E-Mail: raceform@raceform.co.uk
> Web site: http://www.raceform.co.uk

Racing System Builder (RSB)
Professional edition enables you to do sire and damsire research, while their new RSB (fast) edition lets you research more variables at greater speed.

> RSB, Upper Buckenhill Farmhouse, Fownhope,
> Herefordshire. HR1 4PU.
> Tel: 01432 860864
> E-Mail: tmd@racedata.kc3ltd.co.uk
> Web: http://www.racedata.demon.co.uk

Profile (Racehorses & Sires)
500 page book that covers all horses in training, highlighting their likes and dislikes. Useful sires section at the back. Also available on disk.

> Nomadic Press, The Courthouse, Erfstadt Court, Denmark Street,
> Wokingham, Berkshire. RG11 2AY.

James Underwood's European Racing & Breeding Digest
A weekly report on performances and pedigrees in the British Isles and other European countries. Subscribers also receive excellent 'Review' at the season's end.

> European Racing and Breeding Digest, 94 Cornwall Gardens,
> London. SW7 4AX. Tel: 0171 589 0625

Steve Taplin's Guide to Two Year Olds (Annual)
Very useful source of information, giving detailed breeding notes for unraced two-year-olds. Stallion reference section at the back.

> Portway Press Ltd, Halifax, West Yorkshire, HX1 1XE.
> Tel: 01422 330330

Form Sires

Resources on the Internet

The British Racing Centre

Find out the three-generation pedigree of any horse in training. Plus extended pedigrees for most sires past and present. Full racecards and results service too.

Subscription hotline: Tel: 0113 234 2550

Web: http://www.racing.press.net/

Albin Warth's Thoroughbred Pedigree Query

Find out the four-generation pedigree of most sires and damsires. Dosage information giving profile and index.

Web: http://owl.frontier.com/pedigree/

Dr Steve Roman's Web Site

Find out all you ever wanted to know about dosage from the creator of the dosage index. Lots of facts and figures, and some nice pictures too.

Web: http://www.chef-de-race.com/

Hiflyer Magazine (USA)

A Website which hold a selection of interesting articles relating to sires and breeding.

Web: http://www.hiflyer.com/index.html

Daily Racing Form (USA)

A section of these pages is dedicated to showing you how to pick winners. With an interesting piece on pedigree handicapping.

Web: http://slewpy.drf.com/handicapping/picking.html

Form Sires

Chapter 18

Index & Dosage Figures

*Dosage information generated from the site of Albin Warth (http://owl.frontier.com/pedigree/) and based on Steve Roman's list of Chefs de Race

SIRE	SIRES-SIRE	YoB	PROFILE	DI	CD
Alleged	Hoist The Flag	74	9-11-27-4-7	1.37	0.19
Alzao	Lyphard	80	14-11-30-1-0	2.50	0.60
Anshan	Persian Bold	87	5-3-2-4-0	1.80	0.64
Aragon	Mummy's Pet	80	12-0-0-0-0	0.00	2.00
Arazi	Blushing Groom	89	22-1-15-0-10	1.74	0.52
Archway	Thatching	88	8-2-11-0-1	2.38	0.73
Bairn	Northern Baby	82	6-9-12-5-2	1.62	0.35
Ballacashtal	Vice Regent	77	5-1-12-0-0	2.00	0.61
Ballad Rock	Bold Lad (IRE)	74	11-4-3-2-2	3.00	0.91
Batshoof	Sadler's Wells	86	18-4-12-0-0	4.67	1.18
Be My Chief	Chief's Crown	87	8-14-14-0-0	4.14	0.83
Be My Guest	Northern Dancer	74	20-9-15-0-0	4.87	1.11
Bering	Arctic Tern	83	5-3-14-8-6	0.71	-0.19
Beveled	Sharpen Up	82	11-8-14-1-0	3.25	0.85
Bluebird	Storm Bird	84	6-9-13-0-0	3.31	0.75
Broken Hearted	Dara Monarch	84	2-0-4-0-8	0.40	-0.86
Cadeaux Genereux	Young Generation	85	6-1-7-0-2	1.91	0.56
Caerleon	Nijinsky	80	8-4-22-18-0	0.79	0.04
Clantime	Music Boy	81	8-0-0-0-0	0.00	2.00
Common Grounds	Kris	85	8-1-15-4-2	1.22	0.30
Cyrano De Bergerac	Bold Lad (IRE)	83	11-4-3-2-2	3.00	0.91
Damister	Mr Prospector	82	24-8-18-0-0	4.56	1.12
Danehill	Danzig	86	5-13-32-0-2	1.89	0.37
Danzig	Northern Dancer	77	15-11-14-0-0	4.71	1.02
Darshaan	Shirley Heights	81	4-5-4-5-0	1.57	0.44
Dashing Blade	Elegant Air	81	10-7-8-1-0	4.20	1.00
Dayjur	Danzig	87	13-13-22-2-0	2.85	0.74
Diesis	Sharpen Up	80	11-4-11-4-6	1.32	0.28
Distant Relative	Habitat	86	25-7-7-1-4	4.18	1.09
Distinctly North	Minshaanshu Amad	88	14-4-7-0-1	4.78	1.15
Dixieland Band	Northern Dancer	80	13-7-16-0-0	3.50	0.92
Dominion	Derring-Do	72	10-0-2-0-0	11.00	1.67
Don't Forget Me	Ahonoora	84	4-0-0-0-0	0.00	2.00
Doulab	Topsider	82	11-4-6-5-0	2.25	0.81
Dowsing	Riverman	84	20-20-21-1-0	4.39	0.95

Form Sires

Doyoun	Mill Reef	85	11-6-15-10-0	1.40	0.43
Efisio	Formidable	82	5-2-20-0-1	1.55	0.36
El Gran Senor	Northern Dancer	81	11-9-28-0-0	2.43	0.65
Ela-Mana-Mou	Pitcairn	76	6-4-4-0-4	2.00	0.22
Elmaamul	Diesis	87	5-3-18-2-2	1.31	0.23
Emarati	Danzig	86	9-16-14-1-0	4.00	0.82
Fairy King	Northern Dancer	82	12-8-22-0-0	2.82	0.76
Fayruz	Song	83	4-0-0-0-0	0.00	2.00
Formidable	Forli	75	12-6-26-0-2	2.07	0.57
Forzando	Formidable	81	8-2-16-0-0	2.25	0.69
Generous	Caerleon	88	4-1-8-9-0	0.69	0.00
Gone West	Mr Prospector	84	24-14-19-1-0	4.52	1.05
Great Commotion	Nureyev	86	6-1-29-0-0	1.48	0.36
Green Dancer	Nijinsky	72	9-1-22-8-2	1.00	0.17
Green Desert	Danzig	83	10-20-22-0-0	3.73	0.77
Groom Dancer	Blushing Groom	84	19-0-21-0-4	2.03	0.68
Hadeer	General Assembly	82	4-11-7-2-14	0.95	-0.29
High Estate	Shirley Heights	86	10-4-5-5-0	2.20	0.79
Imp Society	Barrera	81	9-6-13-0-0	3.31	0.86
Imperial Frontier	Lyphard	84	14-3-29-0-4	1.70	0.46
In The Wings	Sadler's Wells	86	6-2-13-3-0	1.53	0.46
Indian Ridge	Ahonoora	85	2-2-0-0-0	0.00	1.50
Interrex	Vice Regent	84	11-9-14-2-0	3.00	0.81
Irish River	Riverman	76	10-16-13-1-0	4.33	0.88
Kahyasi	Ile De Bourbon	85	8-0-10-4-6	0.87	0.00
Kalaglow	Kalamoun	78	9-0-7-4-2	1.32	0.45
Keen	Sharpen Up	81	11-4-11-4-6	1.32	0.28
Kefaah	Blushing Groom	85	22-0-16-0-8	1.88	0.61
Known Fact	In Reality	77	16-6-12-2-0	3.50	1.00
Komaite	Nureyev	83	5-3-31-1-0	1.42	0.30
Kris	Sharpen Up	76	11-4-11-4-6	1.32	0.28
Lahib	Riverman	88	10-16-19-1-0	3.38	0.76
Last Tycoon	Try My Best	83	10-5-16-5-0	1.77	0.56
Lear Fan	Roberto	81	8-4-32-2-0	1.56	0.39
Lugana Beach	Tumble Wind	86	2-0-2-0-2	1.00	0.00
Lycius	Mr Prospector	88	25-6-25-0-0	3.48	1.00
Machiavellian	Mr Prospector	87	25-10-24-0-1	3.62	0.97
Manila	Lyphard	83	15-3-24-0-12	1.25	0.17
Marju	Last Tycoon	88	5-2-6-7-2	0.83	0.05
Mazilier	Lyphard	84	13-1-26-0-0	2.08	0.68
Most Welcome	Be My Guest	84	18-4-10-4-0	3.00	1.00
Mr Prospector	Raise A Native	70	23-12-13-4-0	3.95	1.04
Mtoto	Busted	83	2-0-3-1-22	0.14	-1.46
Mujadil	Storm Bird	88	9-8-12-1-0	3.29	0.83

Form Sires

Mujtahid	Woodman	88	14-6-15-7-0	1.90	0.64
Mystiko	Secreto	88	12-4-12-0-2	2.75	0.80
Nashwan	Blushing Groom	86	15-0-9-0-6	1.86	0.60
Never So Bold	Bold Lad (IRE)	80	20-7-3-2-2	5.18	1.21
Night Shift	Northern Dancer	80	11-7-14-0-0	3.57	0.91
Nomination	Dominion	83	4-1-1-2-0	2.20	0.88
Nordico	Northern Dancer	81	15-12-17-2-2	2.84	0.75
Nureyev	Northern Dancer	77	14-7-23-0-0	2.83	0.80
Old Vic	Sadler's Wells	86	9-1-10-0-2	2.14	0.68
Pennine Walk	Persian Bold	82	4-2-4-6-0	1.00	0.25
Persian Bold	Bold Lad (IRE)	75	12-4-2-12-2	1.13	0.38
Petorius	Mummy's Pet	81	10-0-2-0-0	11.00	1.67
Petoski	Niniski	82	4-4-15-4-7	0.84	-0.18
Pharly	Lyphard	74	11-1-26-0-2	1.67	0.47
Polar Falcon	Nureyev	87	5-1-28-0-0	1.43	0.32
Polish Patriot	Danzig	88	8-12-16-0-2	2.80	0.63
Polish Precedent	Danzig	86	6-14-26-0-0	2.54	0.57
Primo Dominie	Dominion	82	10-4-0-0-0	0.00	1.71
Prince Sabo	Young Generation	82	4-0-2-0-0	5.00	1.33
Priolo	Sovereign Dancer	87	11-8-11-2-2	2.58	0.71
Puissance	Thatching	86	8-0-4-0-0	5.00	1.33
Pursuit Of Love	Groom Dancer	89	8-2-12-2-2	1.60	0.46
Rainbow Quest	Blushing Groom	81	19-1-16-4-8	1.40	0.40
Rambo Dancer	Northern Dancer	84	15-12-15-0-0	4.60	1.00
Red Ransom	Roberto	87	9-8-33-2-0	1.81	0.46
Red Sunset	Red God	79	12-5-9-6-0	2.05	0.72
Reprimand	Mummy's Pet	85	11-0-1-0-0	23.00	1.83
Risk Me	Sharpo	84	4-2-9-0-11	0.68	-0.46
Riverman	Never Bend	69	20-16-17-3-0	3.87	0.95
Robellino	Roberto	78	10-7-29-1-1	1.91	0.50
Rock City	Ballad Rock	87	7-6-5-2-2	2.38	0.64
Roi Danzig	Danzig	86	6-20-22-2-0	2.85	0.60
Rousillon	Riverman	81	14-16-15-1-0	4.41	0.93
Royal Academy	Nijinsky	87	9-3-16-8-0	1.25	0.36
Rudimentary	Nureyev	88	5-1-26-4-6	0.83	-0.12
Saddlers' Hall	Sadler's Wells	88	5-1-20-0-2	1.33	0.25
Sadler's Wells	Northern Dancer	81	12-8-22-0-0	2.82	0.76
Safawan	Young Generation	86	13-3-4-0-0	9.00	1.45
Salse	Topsider	85	10-4-19-7-0	1.42	0.43
Salt Dome	Blushing Groom	83	19-0-9-0-4	2.76	0.94
Sayf El Arab	Drone	80	8-12-11-3-0	3.00	0.74
Selkirk	Sharpen Up	88	11-4-11-0-0	3.73	1.00
Shaadi	Danzig	86	11-15-19-0-3	2.84	0.65
Shalford	Thatching	88	6-2-4-0-0	5.00	1.17

Form Sires

Shareef Dancer	Northern Dancer	80	12-16-20-0-0	3.55	0.80
Sharpo	Sharpen Up	77	15-6-11-0-0	4.82	1.13
Sharrood	Caro	83	10-8-8-0-4	2.75	0.67
Shavian	Kris	87	10-1-11-6-2	1.22	0.37
Shirley Heights	Mill Reef	75	9-6-13-10-0	1.30	0.37
Silver Hawk	Roberto	79	8-6-30-0-2	1.71	0.39
Slip Anchor	Shirley Heights	82	4-3-6-7-0	1.00	0.20
Soviet Lad	Nureyev	85	9-1-32-0-2	1.44	0.34
Soviet Star	Nureyev	84	5-1-26-0-4	1.12	0.08
Statoblest	Ahonoora	86	2-0-0-0-0	0.00	2.00
Storm Cat	Storm Bird	83	11-8-10-1-0	4.00	0.97
Superlative	Nebbiolo	81	2-0-0-0-0	0.00	2.00
Taufan	Stop The Music	77	4-4-14-0-0	2.14	0.55
Thatching	Thatch	75	12-2-10-0-0	3.80	1.08
Timeless Times	Timeless Moment	88	6-10-16-0-0	3.00	0.69
Tina's Pet	Mummy's Pet	78	15-0-1-0-0	31.00	1.88
Tirol	Thatching	87	6-0-6-0-0	3.00	1.00
Tragic Role	Nureyev	86	5-3-38-4-2	1.08	0.10
Treasure Kay	Mummy's Pet	83	12-0-2-0-0	13.00	1.71
Try My Best	Northern Dancer	75	11-9-28-0-0	2.43	0.65
Unfuwain	Northern Dancer	85	11-7-14-0-2	2.78	0.74
Waajib	Known Fact	85	13-6-21-0-0	2.81	0.80
Warrshan	Northern Dancer	86	11-8-27-4-2	1.67	0.42
Weldnaas	Diesis	86	6-4-12-2-2	1.60	0.38
Woodman	Mr Prospector	83	20-10-26-0-0	3.31	0.89
Zilzal	Nureyev	86	6-2-26-0-12	0.84	-0.22

Form Sires

Form Sires

Efisio	Formidable	82	5-2-20-0-1	1.55	0.36
Forzando	Formidable	81	8-2-16-0-0	2.25	0.69
Hadeer	General Assembly	82	4-11-7-2-14	0.95	-0.29
Pursuit Of Love	Groom Dancer	89	8-2-12-2-2	1.60	0.46
Distant Relative	Habitat	86	25-7-7-1-4	4.18	1.09
Alleged	Hoist The Flag	74	9-11-27-4-7	1.37	0.19
Kahyasi	Ile De Bourbon	85	8-0-10-4-6	0.87	0.00
Known Fact	In Reality	77	16-6-12-2-0	3.50	1.00
Kalaglow	Kalamoun	78	9-0-7-4-2	1.32	0.45
Warning	Known Fact	85	13-6-21-0-0	2.81	0.80
Common Grounds	Kris	85	8-1-15-4-2	1.22	0.30
Shavian	Kris	87	10-1-11-6-2	1.22	0.37
Marju	Last Tycoon	88	5-2-6-7-2	0.83	0.05
Alzao	Lyphard	80	14-11-30-1-0	2.50	0.60
Imperial Frontier	Lyphard	84	14-3-29-0-4	1.70	0.46
Manila	Lyphard	83	15-3-24-0-12	1.25	0.17
Mazilier	Lyphard	84	13-1-26-0-0	2.08	0.68
Pharly	Lyphard	74	11-1-26-0-2	1.67	0.47
Doyoun	Mill Reef	85	11-6-15-10-0	1.40	0.43
Shirley Heights	Mill Reef	75	9-6-13-10-0	1.30	0.37
Distinctly North	Minshaanshu Amad	88	14-4-7-0-1	4.78	1.15
Damister	Mr Prospector	82	24-8-18-0-0	4.56	1.12
Gone West	Mr Prospector	84	24-14-19-1-0	4.52	1.05
Lycius	Mr Prospector	88	25-6-25-0-0	3.48	1.00
Machiavellian	Mr Prospector	87	25-10-24-0-1	3.62	0.97
Woodman	Mr Prospector	83	20-10-26-0-0	3.31	0.89
Aragon	Mummy's Pet	80	12-0-0-0-0	0.00	2.00
Petorius	Mummy's Pet	81	10-0-2-0-0	11.00	1.67
Reprimand	Mummy's Pet	85	11-0-1-0-0	23.00	1.83
Tina's Pet	Mummy's Pet	78	15-0-1-0-0	31.00	1.88
Treasure Kay	Mummy's Pet	83	12-0-2-0-0	13.00	1.71
Clantime	Music Boy	81	8-0-0-0-0	0.00	2.00
Superlative	Nebbiolo	81	2-0-0-0-0	0.00	2.00
Riverman	Never Bend	69	20-16-17-3-0	3.87	0.95
Caerleon	Nijinsky	80	8-4-22-18-0	0.79	0.04
Green Dancer	Nijinsky	72	9-1-22-8-2	1.00	0.17
Royal Academy	Nijinsky	87	9-3-16-8-0	1.25	0.36
Petoski	Niniski	82	4-4-15-4-7	0.84	-0.18
Bairn	Northern Baby	82	6-9-12-5-2	1.62	0.35
Be My Guest	Northern Dancer	74	20-9-15-0-0	4.87	1.11
Danzig	Northern Dancer	77	15-11-14-0-0	4.71	1.02
Dixieland Band	Northern Dancer	80	13-7-16-0-0	3.50	0.92
El Gran Senor	Northern Dancer	81	11-9-28-0-0	2.43	0.65
Fairy King	Northern Dancer	82	12-8-22-0-0	2.82	0.76

Form Sires

Night Shift	Northern Dancer	80	11-7-14-0-0	3.57	0.91
Nordico	Northern Dancer	81	15-12-17-2-2	2.84	0.75
Nureyev	Northern Dancer	77	14-7-23-0-0	2.83	0.80
Rambo Dancer	Northern Dancer	84	15-12-15-0-0	4.60	1.00
Sadler's Wells	Northern Dancer	81	12-8-22-0-0	2.82	0.76
Shareef Dancer	Northern Dancer	80	12-16-20-0-0	3.55	0.80
Try My Best	Northern Dancer	75	11-9-28-0-0	2.43	0.65
Unfuwain	Northern Dancer	85	11-7-14-0-2	2.78	0.74
Warrshan	Northern Dancer	86	11-8-27-4-2	1.67	0.42
Great Commotion	Nureyev	86	6-1-29-0-0	1.48	0.36
Komaite	Nureyev	83	5-3-31-1-0	1.42	0.30
Polar Falcon	Nureyev	87	5-1-28-0-0	1.43	0.32
Rudimentary	Nureyev	88	5-1-26-4-6	0.83	-0.12
Soviet Lad	Nureyev	85	9-1-32-0-2	1.44	0.34
Soviet Star	Nureyev	84	5-1-26-0-4	1.12	0.08
Tragic Role	Nureyev	86	5-3-38-4-2	1.08	0.10
Zilzal	Nureyev	86	6-2-26-0-12	0.84	-0.22
Anshan	Persian Bold	87	5-3-2-4-0	1.80	0.64
Pennine Walk	Persian Bold	82	4-2-4-6-0	1.00	0.25
Ela-Mana-Mou	Pitcairn	76	6-4-4-0-4	2.00	0.22
Mr Prospector	Raise A Native	70	23-12-13-4-0	3.95	1.04
Red Sunset	Red God	79	12-5-9-6-0	2.05	0.72
Dowsing	Riverman	84	20-20-21-1-0	4.39	0.95
Irish River	Riverman	76	10-16-13-1-0	4.33	0.88
Lahib	Riverman	88	10-16-19-1-0	3.38	0.76
Rousillon	Riverman	81	14-16-15-1-0	4.41	0.93
Lear Fan	Roberto	81	8-4-32-2-0	1.56	0.39
Red Ransom	Roberto	87	9-8-33-2-0	1.81	0.46
Robellino	Roberto	78	10-7-29-1-1	1.91	0.50
Silver Hawk	Roberto	79	8-6-30-0-2	1.71	0.39
Batshoof	Sadler's Wells	86	18-4-12-0-0	4.67	1.18
In The Wings	Sadler's Wells	86	6-2-13-3-0	1.53	0.46
Old Vic	Sadler's Wells	86	9-1-10-0-2	2.14	0.68
Saddlers' Hall	Sadler's Wells	88	5-1-20-0-2	1.33	0.25
Mystiko	Secreto	88	12-4-12-0-2	2.75	0.80
Beveled	Sharpen Up	82	11-8-14-1-0	3.25	0.85
Diesis	Sharpen Up	80	11-4-11-4-6	1.32	0.28
Keen	Sharpen Up	81	11-4-11-4-6	1.32	0.28
Kris	Sharpen Up	76	11-4-11-4-6	1.32	0.28
Selkirk	Sharpen Up	88	11-4-11-0-0	3.73	1.00
Sharpo	Sharpen Up	77	15-6-11-0-0	4.82	1.13
Risk Me	Sharpo	84	4-2-9-0-11	0.68	-0.46
Darshaan	Shirley Heights	81	4-5-4-5-0	1.57	0.44
High Estate	Shirley Heights	86	10-4-5-5-0	2.20	0.79

Form Sires

Slip Anchor	Shirley Heights	82	4-3-6-7-0	1.00	0.20
Fayruz	Song	83	4-0-0-0-0	0.00	2.00
Priolo	Sovereign Dancer	87	11-8-11-2-2	2.58	0.71
Taufan	Stop The Music	77	4-4-14-0-0	2.14	0.55
Bluebird	Storm Bird	84	6-9-13-0-0	3.31	0.75
Mujadil	Storm Bird	88	9-8-12-1-0	3.29	0.83
Storm Cat	Storm Bird	83	11-8-10-1-0	4.00	0.97
Thatching	Thatch	75	12-2-10-0-0	3.80	1.08
Archway	Thatching	88	8-2-11-0-1	2.38	0.73
Puissance	Thatching	86	8-0-4-0-0	5.00	1.33
Shalford	Thatching	88	6-2-4-0-0	5.00	1.17
Tirol	Thatching	87	6-0-6-0-0	3.00	1.00
Timeless Times	Timeless Moment	88	6-10-16-0-0	3.00	0.69
Doulab	Topsider	82	11-4-6-5-0	2.25	0.81
Salse	Topsider	85	10-4-19-7-0	1.42	0.43
Last Tycoon	Try My Best	83	10-5-16-5-0	1.77	0.56
Waajib	Try My Best	83	5-2-12-0-3	1.44	0.27
Lugana Beach	Tumble Wind	86	2-0-2-0-2	1.00	0.00
Ballacashtal	Vice Regent	77	5-1-12-0-0	2.00	0.61
Interrex	Vice Regent	84	11-9-14-2-0	3.00	0.81
Mujtahid	Woodman	88	14-6-15-7-0	1.90	0.64
Cadeaux Genereux	Young Generation	85	6-1-7-0-2	1.91	0.56
Prince Sabo	Young Generation	82	4-0-2-0-0	5.00	1.33
Safawan	Young Generation	86	13-3-4-0-0	9.00	1.45

Form Sires

Form Sires

Hot Spark	Habitat	72	27-7-5-3-0	6.64	1.38
Hotfoot	Firestreak	63	14-6-10-0-2	3.57	0.94
Ile De Bourbon	Nijinsky	75	5-1-16-8-0	0.88	0.10
Indian King	Raja Baba	78	13-9-5-3-0	4.45	1.07
Irish River	Riverman	76	10-16-13-1-0	4.33	0.88
Kalaglow	Kalamoun	78	9-0-7-4-2	1.32	0.45
Key To The Mint	Graustark	69	1-4-27-14-4	0.59	-0.32
Kings Lake	Nijinsky	78	5-4-16-13-6	0.63	-0.25
Known Fact	In Reality	77	16-6-12-2-0	3.50	1.00
Kris	Sharpen Up	76	11-4-11-4-6	1.32	0.28
Lochnager	Dumbarnie	72	6-6-4-0-4	2.33	0.50
Lomond	Northern Dancer	80	13-8-14-5-0	2.33	0.73
Lord Gayle	Sir Gaylord	65	25-14-15-2-4	3.44	0.90
Luthier	Klairon	65	0-6-11-0-5	1.10	-0.18
Lyphard	Northern Dancer	69	25-7-14-0-2	4.33	1.10
Main Reef	Mill Reef	76	11-6-13-10-2	1.27	0.33
Majestic Light	Majestic Prince	73	13-4-10-0-5	2.20	0.63
Mill Reef	Never Bend	68	19-16-12-5-0	3.73	0.94
Miswaki	Mr Prospector	78	20-10-28-2-0	2.75	0.80
Mount Hagen	Bold Bidder	71	13-17-17-5-0	2.85	0.73
Mr Prospector	Raise A Native	70	23-12-13-4-0	3.95	1.04
Mummy's Pet	Sing Sing	68	26-0-2-0-0	27.00	1.86
Music Boy	Jukebox	73	4-0-0-2-2	1.00	0.25
Nebbiolo	Yellow God	74	7-0-1-0-0	15.00	1.75
Night Shift	Northern Dancer	80	11-7-14-0-0	3.57	0.91
Nijinsky	Northern Dancer	67	13-7-20-0-0	3.00	0.82
Niniski	Nijinsky	76	6-4-22-8-6	0.84	-0.09
Nonoalco	Nearctic	71	10-8-10-2-0	3.29	0.87
Northern Dancer	Nearctic	61	8-16-15-3-0	3.00	0.69
Northfields	Northern Dancer	68	15-7-16-2-0	3.00	0.88
Nureyev	Northern Dancer	77	14-7-23-0-0	2.83	0.80
Pas De Seul	Mill Reef	79	10-6-18-10-0	1.32	0.36
Persian Bold	Bold Lad (IRE)	75	12-4-2-12-2	1.13	0.38
Pharly	Lyphard	74	11-1-26-0-2	1.67	0.47
Rainbow Quest	Blushing Groom	81	19-1-16-4-8	1.40	0.40
Rarity	Hethersett	67	1-8-5-9-5	0.70	-0.32
Red Alert	Red God	71	14-2-3-1-0	7.00	1.45
Red Sunset	Red God	79	12-5-9-6-0	2.05	0.72
Reform	Pall Mall	64	7-0-15-0-6	1.07	0.07
Relkino	Relko	73	1-4-8-20-1	0.36	-0.47
Riverman	Never Bend	69	20-16-17-3-0	3.87	0.95
Roberto	Hail To Reason	69	16-8-32-0-2	2.22	0.62
Rousillon	Riverman	81	14-16-15-1-0	4.41	0.93
Runnett	Mummy's Pet	77	16-2-0-0-0	0.00	1.89

Form Sires

Sadler's Wells	Northern Dancer	81	12-8-22-0-0	2.82	0.76
Sallust	Pall Mall	69	6-2-0-0-0	0.00	1.75
Seattle Slew	Bold Reasoning	74	7-6-4-5-0	2.14	0.68
Secretariat	Bold Ruler	70	20-14-7-9-0	3.00	0.90
Secreto	Northern Dancer	81	17-15-22-2-0	3.31	0.84
Shareef Dancer	Northern Dancer	80	12-16-22-0-0	3.55	0.80
Sharpen Up	Atan	69	6-8-8-2-0	3.00	0.75
Shirley Heights	Mill Reef	75	9-6-13-10-0	1.30	0.37
Sir Ivor	Sir Gaylord	65	11-16-16-5-2	2.33	0.58
Song	Sing Sing	66	11-0-3-0-0	8.33	1.57
Star Appeal	Appiani II	70	1-0-7-6-4	0.33	-0.67
Storm Bird	Northern Dancer	78	11-7-16-0-0	3.25	0.85
Teenoso	Youth	80	4-5-9-8-0	1.08	0.19
Thatching	Thatch	75	12-2-10-0-0	3.80	1.08
The Minstrel	Northern Dancer	74	11-7-16-0-0	3.25	0.85
Top Ville	High Top	76	5-0-23-4-2	0.94	0.06
Topsider	Northern Dancer	74	20-9-17-10-0	2.03	0.70
Troy	Petingo	76	13-8-5-0-6	2.76	0.69
Try My Best	Northern Dancer	75	11-9-28-0-0	2.43	0.65
Vaguely Noble	Vienna	65	9-10-21-0-2	2.36	0.57
Vice Regent	Northern Dancer	67	13-7-14-0-0	3.86	0.97
Welsh Pageant	Tudor Melody	66	24-0-2-0-6	3.57	1.13
Welsh Saint	St Paddy	66	17-0-13-6-2	1.62	0.63

Form Sires

Form Sires

Dancing Brave	Lyphard	83	12-5-25-0-0	2.36	0.69
Pharly	Lyphard	74	11-1-26-0-2	1.67	0.47
Majestic Light	Majestic Prince	73	13-4-10-0-5	2.20	0.63
Main Reef	Mill Reef	76	11-6-13-10-2	1.27	0.33
Pas De Seul	Mill Reef	79	10-6-18-10-0	1.32	0.36
Shirley Heights	Mill Reef	75	9-6-13-10-0	1.30	0.37
Fappiano	Mr Prospector	77	18-7-14-1-0	4.00	1.05
Miswaki	Mr Prospector	78	20-10-28-2-0	2.75	0.80
Runnett	Mummy's Pet	77	16-2-0-0-0	0.00	1.89
Nonoalco	Nearctic	71	10-8-10-2-0	3.29	0.87
Northern Dancer	Nearctic	61	8-16-15-3-0	3.00	0.69
Mill Reef	Never Bend	68	19-16-12-5-0	3.73	0.94
Riverman	Never Bend	69	20-16-17-3-0	3.87	0.95
Caerleon	Nijinsky	80	8-4-22-18-0	0.79	0.04
Green Dancer	Nijinsky	72	9-1-22-8-2	1.00	0.17
Ile De Bourbon	Nijinsky	75	5-1-16-8-0	0.88	0.10
Kings Lake	Nijinsky	78	5-4-16-13-6	0.63	-0.25
Niniski	Nijinsky	76	6-4-22-8-6	0.84	-0.09
Be My Guest	Northern Dancer	74	20-9-15-0-0	4.87	1.11
Dance In Time	Northern Dancer	74	11-7-14-0-0	3.57	0.91
Danzig	Northern Dancer	77	15-11-14-0-0	4.71	1.02
Lomond	Northern Dancer	80	13-8-14-5-0	2.33	0.73
Lyphard	Northern Dancer	69	25-7-14-0-2	4.33	1.10
Night Shift	Northern Dancer	80	11-7-14-0-0	3.57	0.91
Nijinsky	Northern Dancer	67	13-7-20-0-0	3.00	0.82
Northfields	Northern Dancer	68	15-7-16-2-0	3.00	0.88
Nureyev	Northern Dancer	77	14-7-23-0-0	2.83	0.80
Sadler's Wells	Northern Dancer	81	12-8-22-0-0	2.82	0.76
Secreto	Northern Dancer	81	17-15-22-2-0	3.31	0.84
Shareef Dancer	Northern Dancer	80	12-16-22-0-0	3.55	0.80
Storm Bird	Northern Dancer	78	11-7-16-0-0	3.25	0.85
The Minstrel	Northern Dancer	74	11-7-16-0-0	3.25	0.85
Topsider	Northern Dancer	74	20-9-17-10-0	2.03	0.70
Try My Best	Northern Dancer	75	11-9-28-0-0	2.43	0.65
Vice Regent	Northern Dancer	67	13-7-14-0-0	3.86	0.97
Reform	Pall Mall	64	7-0-15-0-6	1.07	0.07
Sallust	Pall Mall	69	6-2-0-0-0	0.00	1.75
Troy	Petingo	76	13-8-5-0-6	2.76	0.69
Ela-Mana-Mou	Pitcairn	76	6-4-4-0-4	2.00	0.44
Bay Express	Polyfoto	71	8-0-2-0-0	9.00	1.60
Exclusive Native	Raise A Native	65	16-10-10-4-0	3.44	0.95
Mr Prospector	Raise A Native	70	23-12-13-4-0	3.95	1.04
Indian King	Raja Baba	78	13-9-5-3-0	4.45	1.07
Blushing Groom	Red God	74	16-2-5-1-10	1.52	0.38

Form Sires

Red Alert	Red God	71	14-2-3-1-0	7.00	1.45
Red Sunset	Red God	79	12-5-9-6-0	2.05	0.72
Relkino	Relko	73	1-4-8-20-1	0.36	-0.47
Irish River	Riverman	76	10-16-13-1-0	4.33	0.88
Rousillon	Riverman	81	14-16-15-1-0	4.41	0.93
Artaius	Round Table	74	14-8-9-20-1	1.04	0.27
Arctic Tern	Sea-Bird II	73	2-8-13-19-0	0.65	-0.17
General Assembly	Secretariat	76	9-23-18-6-0	2.73	0.63
Diesis	Sharpen Up	80	11-4-11-4-6	1.32	0.28
Kris	Sharpen Up	76	11-4-11-4-6	1.32	0.28
Darshaan	Shirley Heights	81	4-5-4-5-0	1.57	0.44
Mummy's Pet	Sing Sing	68	26-0-2-0-0	27.00	1.86
Song	Sing Sing	66	11-0-3-0-0	8.33	1.57
Habitat	Sir Gaylord	66	13-14-13-4-2	2.68	0.70
Lord Gayle	Sir Gaylord	65	25-14-15-2-4	3.44	0.90
Sir Ivor	Sir Gaylord	65	11-16-16-5-2	2.33	0.58
Welsh Saint	St Paddy	66	17-0-13-6-2	1.62	0.63
Thatching	Thatch	75	12-2-10-0-0	3.80	1.08
Frimley Park	Tribal Chief	75	10-4-2-0-2	5.00	1.11
Welsh Pageant	Tudor Melody	66	24-0-2-0-6	3.57	1.13
Vaguely Noble	Vienna	65	9-10-21-0-2	2.36	0.57
Nebbiolo	Yellow God	74	7-0-1-0-0	15.00	1.75
Teenoso	Youth	80	4-5-9-8-0	1.08	0.19